The Art of
WOOD CARVING

The author finishing a design for a 48 inch Bremen Eagle and Banner. This is where all the work shown in the following pages begins—on the drafting board. (*Courtesy Maine Coast Fisherman*)

The Art of
WOOD CARVING

by

JOHN UPTON

D. VAN NOSTRAND COMPANY, INC.

PRINCETON, NEW JERSEY

TORONTO   LONDON

Van Nostrand Regional Offices: *New York, Chicago, San Francisco*

D. Van Nostrand Company, Ltd., *London*

D. Van Nostrand Company (Canada), Ltd., *Toronto*

Library of Congress Catalog Card No. 58-14222

First Published, October 1958
*Reprinted, April 1959, May 1961,
June 1965, March 1967*

PRINTED IN THE UNITED STATES OF AMERICA

Preface

Names and probable dates and places are known about many of the past master wood carvers such as the Skillins of New York, Samuel McIntire of Salem, Massachusetts, Benjamin Rush of Philadelphia, William Southworth of Portland and Newcastle, Maine, and John H. Bellamy of Kittery, Maine, but to my knowledge there are few books of instructions on the subject. What few I have seen start off with the assumption that the reader has served a long apprenticeship in the art and is at least a journeyman. If you are neither an apprentice nor a journeyman, but a person like myself who loves wood and tools, has some small skill with a pencil and a few carving tools, what follows in this "effort to explain" may be of interest.

The history of wood carving is more or less unwritten in words but not in deeds. Probably the greatest wood carver of any time was Grinling Gibbons of England. I have seen many pictures of his work but, to my knowledge, have never seen any of the originals. How he did all the work accredited to him in one lifetime, I cannot know. We think in terms of religious carvings when we think of the history of the art. Probably for the reason there are more churches extant than other structures in which the carved forms were used to add warmth and beauty to the cold of stone and mortar.

The oldest example we have of ship carving is the Viking ship. In imagination we must perforce pass through the years to such figureheads as have been preserved from the past, in drawings from the British Admiralty, in records of our own Naval Service and some works and drawings that have come down to us almost by error. The field of marine carving is most aptly covered by Pauline A. Pinckney in her book, "American Figureheads and Their Carvers," and there is a good collection in the Marine Museum at Mystic, Connecticut.

Some of the fine examples of ecclesiastical carvings are shown as incidental parts of illustrations in Gerald Cobb's "The Old Churches of London."

"The Index of American Design," edited by Erwin O. Christensen, has a lot of valuable illustrations and data on Early American wood carvings. Another valuable source of information is "The Encyclopedia of Furniture" by Joseph Aronson. There are many other sources of information that can be found in most urban libraries, but, withal, the bibliography in the field of wood carving is not extensive.

Before finishing these preliminary remarks, it may not be out of place to say something about source material. Several of our illustrated weekly or monthly magazines are of invaluable use in this respect. I think that the greatest source of material available is "The National Geographic Magazine." Many of these issues have authoritative information on the subjects you may want to use, such as animals and birds. A well-illustrated dictionary or the Encyclopaedia Britannica is of invaluable use. Advertising illustrations are sometimes extremely good. To save time and effort—let alone frustration—it is a good idea to have a file of envelopes or folders indexed with the subjects that strike your fancy.

Probably the most important factor in the success of a venture in wood carving is a tolerant, skeptical, critical and uncomplaining spouse—one who can, in few words, whittle you and your efforts down to size—and keep you there.

Acknowledgments

I wish to thank all those who have given me permission to use photographs of my work which they own and all the others who have obtained carvings of mine that are not illustrated for lack of room.

Particularly I want to thank my friends and the editors who have given me advice and encouragement in the preparation of this book and for their further interest in its production. I am obliged to Ivan W. Flye for his skill in photographing so well the processes that are illustrated.

Most especially I want to acknowledge the great debt I owe my wife whose patience and fortitude and whose labor in typing have made this book possible.

Contents

CHAPTER   PAGE

1 THE REASON FOR USING WOOD   1

2 WOODS BEST SUITED FOR CARVING   4

3 THE KIND OF TOOLS TO BUY AND USE   13

4 THE WOOD CARVER'S BENCH AND SHOP   29

5 PREPARATION OF THE DRAWING FOR A CARVING   34

6 GETTING OUT THE PARTS AND GLUING   47

7 BOSTING OUT, OR ROUGH CARVING   55

8 DETAIL CARVING   73

9 MAKING A STERN TRANSOM CARVING   87

10 MAKING A CARVED PANEL   101

11 POLYCHROMING, GILDING, AND STAINING   112

GLOSSARY   121

INDEX   127

List of Illustrations

PHOTOGRAPHS

Finishing a design for a 48 inch Bremen Eagle and Banner *Frontispiece*

1   Gilded eagles *Facing page* 1
2   Stern transom—"Rolling Stone IV—Red Bank" 3
3   Paring off profile of design outline 8
4   Native white oak 10
5   American walnut 10
6   Honduras mahogany 11
7   Eastern white pine 11
8   Massive cuts in mahogany 12
9   Long, sweeping cuts in mahogany 12
10   The four tools I commonly use 14
11   Other tools generally used 14
12   A handful of tools 15
13   About one half the tools from a wood carver's chest 15
14   Position of tool on sharpening stone 17
15   Tools in the bench tray 20
16   "A place for everything" 23
17   Work on band saw 24
18   Woodworker's vise on the carving bench 32
19   Detail of bookcase 34
20   Corner cupboard 35
21   Detail of bookcase cornice 37
22   Pair of wall brackets 37
23   A small American Eagle showing parts assembled 39
24   A small American Eagle completed 39
25   This and the next four photographs show processes for completing a Bremen Eagle. The wings and head are bosted out 42
26   The body and wings 42
27   The head and body pad detail-carved 43
28   The elements are assembled 43
29   The completed carving 43
30   "Some people want angels" 45
31   Bull's-eye mirror frame and eagle 45
32   Caduceus carved in alto-relievo 46
33   "Some people want tables" 46

34	Cutting out a piercing on the jigsaw	49
35	Jointing the edge of a 2″ mahogany plank	52
36	Stock in clamps after jointing and gluing up	53
37	Bosting out to stopcut	57
38	Starting the back cuts	58
39	Parts for one of a pair of large American Eagles	59
40	The pair of 4-foot American Eagles	60
41	"No comment"	61
42	The old-fashioned wood jaw and screw clamp in use	62
43	The vise jig in use	64
44	Bosting out with broad gouge	65
45	Finishing off the profile with the spoke shave	66
46	Pierced work	67
47	Pierced work—first step	68
48	Pierced work—second step	68
49	Pierced work—third step	69
50	Pierced work—the completed carving	69
51	Finishing off the sides of a piercing	71
52	Detail of a carved chest	72
53	A carving in the round	74
54	A carving in alto-relievo	74
55	The tools and partly completed detail of the feathering of an eagle	75
56	The steps to develop rope molding	77
57	Two pieces of rope molding	77
58	An American Eagle	78
59	A splendid American Eagle carved by Samuel McIntire	79
60	Bill of Sale for Eagle carved by Samuel McIntire	79
61	Using the skew chisel	80
62	A Bremen Eagle and Banner	81
63	A seagull. Wood sculpture by Charles G. Chase	84
64	An osprey sculptured in black walnut by Charles G. Chase	85
65	A greater yellowlegs sculptured by Charles G. Chase	85
66	An abstract carving in the round	86
67	The eagle is detail-carved	96
68	Name and hailing port banners are checked for fit	97
69	The finished transom	97
70	The Ancient Mariner	98
71	Cutting along the outline of the raising	102
72	Cutting along the saw scarf	103
73	Cutting the raising down	103
74	Stopcutting along the outline	105

75	Backcutting to the stopcuts	105
76	Modeling the leaves	106
77	Finishing the modeling of the sections	107
78	Modeling the edge	108
79	Bookcase showing use of scallop shells	110
80	Mantel and fire frame detail	111
81	A Bremen Eagle	115

FIGURES

2-1	How to fag in a "Dutchman"	4
2-2	To bottom off a carved sinking or section	5
2-3	Making stopcuts	6
3-1	Sharpening a chisel	18
3-2	Sharpening a gouge	19
3-3	The counterbore	21
3-4A	Shapes and names of carving tools	25
3-4B	Slips and stones	26
3-4C	Shapes of cutting edges of carving tools	27
3-4D	Beginner's set	28
3-4E	Rifflers	28
3-4F	Rasp	28
3-4G	Rasp	28
4-1	Plan of work shop	30
4-2A	Plan of work shop, showing carving and side bench	31
4-2B	Isometric drawing of carving bench	31
5-1	Design for a proposed carved eagle	41
6-1	To set a plug	51
7-1	Plan of the hold-down or back-up	55
7-2	The vise jig	63
9-1	Transom curve has been scribed off	87
9-2	Template scribed from transom	88
9-3	Transom is outlined on false transom	88
9-4	Suggested design for transom carving	88
9-5	Suggested design for stern transom carving	89
9-6	Clip stock to length, joint, glue and clamp	89
9-7	Position of block on false transom for scribing	89
9-8	Back cut completed	90
9-9	Checking profiled blank on transom	90
9-10	Carving the design	91
9-11	Making and lettering banners	91
10-1	Layout for pineapple project	100

Photo 1 Gilded eagles. (*Courtesy Patrick Dolan, Mayfair, London*)

1

The Reason for Using Wood

Mankind has always had a dependence on wood. It is the most common substance that we use next to the earth itself. Throughout the years of man's history it has been a potent source of comfort: heat, shelter, tools, benches and transportation. There is hardly a field of activity in which wood does not play a part. What is more natural than for a man to use such a versatile material as a medium in which to express his love of form and line and shape?

In imagination we can go back into the past and see man using wood to his immediate advantage—the first wheel, the first means of water transport, the first fire, the first place to sit off the cold of stone or earth. Even today we can find primitive men using wood for these elemental needs. What is more logical than to expect that man should resort to this most plentiful material as a means of expressing himself in tangible form—a way to embellish things?

In our "sophisticated world" of today we still use wood for many of our comforts. Of course, people who must be "different" won't agree that wood has a place in the field of design, of decoration, of utility. I am old-fashioned enough to think that wood has its place in these fields. How else can we feel—those of us who love wood for its versatility, its beauty, its feel—when we look out of doors and see the beauty in each tree across the field? When people are surrounded by the forests, it is natural to presume that they are inspired to use this common means to tell a story. Give a small boy a jackknife and watch him whittle out "something." Give a man a jackknife and he, too, whittles out "something." Give a wood carver a shaped tool and he also will whittle out "something."

This love of making something of beauty for beauty's sake goes far back into the history of man. Someone has said that beauty is in the eye of the beholder. For my part, I think that beauty is in the

1

eye and mind of the creator, the worker, the artisan who makes things from the material at hand. The results can be called "art," I suppose.

However, I like to think that I make things because I have a small gift of tool manipulation. Other people like the sort of work I do. They call it "art." I call it wood carving and let it go at that. The art of wood carving, then, is a form of expression that lets me use my small skills, imagination, and love of line to express some of the feeling I have for the medium in which I have chosen to work. I let off steam in some of my carvings about the encroachment on our liberties and freedoms by the unthinking and those trying to impose their privilege upon us.

The Viking ships, Phoenician galleys, Roman men-of-war, Chinese junks, American clipper ships and modern yachts are all expressions of men's attempts to use wood for their own purposes. When any of these craft was built, the desire to add something to their undoubted beauty of line inspired the builders to embellish the hulls fore and aft with some greater form of beauty. The stern transoms, the bow and even the catheads were logical places to add bits of fancy work such as scrolls and banners, figureheads and cartouches. The result was not "to gild the lily," but to enhance the already created beauty of the vessel.

There can be humor in the work of wood carvers. Some years ago *Life* magazine had some pictures of two miserere. One was a man beating his wife. I forget the other. Nevertheless, the ancient craftsman who made these two carvings had undoubtedly spent months, probably years, carving pew ends, altar screens, rood screens and the Lord knows what else. Suddenly he made up his mind that there should be some slight bit of levity in the seriousness of his work and where better to hide his humor than under the seat of the mighty?

There are some of us who see beauty in the hard lines of mathematics as expressed in the stark, unadorned lines of our modern architectural forms. I can appreciate the magnificent sweep and curve of the George Washington Bridge, the splendor of the United Nations Buildings, the great sweep of the high, vaulted ceiling of the Cathedral of St. John the Divine. In the Cathedral, however, the mathematical certainty of line and form is warmed and becomes more intimate for me because of the wonderful woodwork that patient hands and years of time have created. Without this warmth and intimacy of a common substance, the starkness of the stone and the mathematics would be awe inspiring but not soul lifting.

Hence, wood to me is the living expression of beauty. What I do to it is tinged with this same feeling. Nature's patient years went into its making. Who are we, in the hurry and bustle of this world, to take other than patient time to say in wood what words fail to say?

Photo 2 Completed stern transom carvings for motor sailer "Rolling Stone IV— Red Bank." (*Courtesy Donald Stone, owner*)

Photo: Dorn's, Red Bank, N. J.

2

Woods Best Suited for Carving

Few of us can pass a fine piece of cabinet work without wanting to rub our hands over the surface if only to assure ourselves that the piece is real and not a bit of our imagination. In so doing we are paying a slight tribute to the beauty of the wood. We may think this is not the reason, but if it isn't, what else can it be? I have a table in my workshop I recently made of mahogany for my use as a writing table. It's been there about ten days and in that time, with only one exception, people who came into the shop have looked at it, caressed

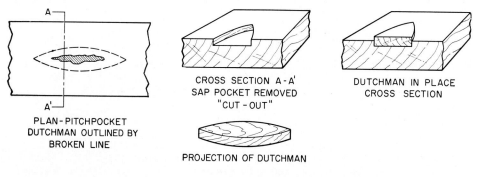

PLAN-PITCHPOCKET
DUTCHMAN OUTLINED BY
BROKEN LINE

CROSS SECTION A-A'
SAP POCKET REMOVED
"CUT-OUT"

DUTCHMAN IN PLACE
CROSS SECTION

PROJECTION OF DUTCHMAN

PROCEDURE

1. Make "Dutchman" large enough to cover sap pocket completely. Make sides square—grain to run in same direction as stock.

2. Scribe around "Dutchman" placed over sap pocket with point of knife.

3. Make back-cut inside scribed line. Remove stock to $\frac{1}{16}$-inch depth less than thickness of "Dutchman." Bottom off. Pare stopcuts to scribed line for press fit.

4. Glue sides of cut-out. Press "Dutchman" in place. Let glue set. Pare off top of "Dutchman." Proceed with carving.

Figure 2-1 HOW TO FAG IN A "DUTCHMAN"

4

the top with their finger tips, and spoken of the beauty of the wood. Never mind the workmanship; that's beside the point. This to me is quite understandable. I do it myself and ponder on the beauty of the grain and wonderful feel of the surface.

Probably the four most common woods used for carving in this country are white pine, white oak, walnut, and mahogany. I have used all four varieties in my work and what I found out about these woods is summarized in the following comments.

White Oak. A coarse-grained, dense, hard wood (Photo 4). Fine detail is difficult to develop in this wood because the alternate layers of hard and soft wood tend to make the tools jump and chatter. The wood is best for large, bold carvings, and its use, to a great extent, is confined to church work. It would be difficult to find a better wood for this purpose for the reason that the massive effects that must be developed in church carvings are best executed in a strong, hard, dependable wood. I have found it difficult to work unless the carving

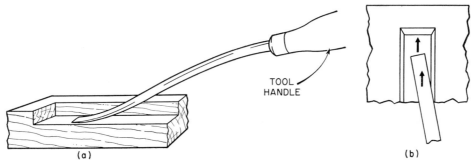

TOOL HANDLE

(a)　　　　　　　　　　　　　　　　　　(b)

PROCEDURE

(a) After stopcuts are completed and stock is removed, to smooth off the bottom of a sinking or carved section, use long bent chisel as shown above.

(b) If cut is across grain, hold chisel so that its cutting edge is at a skew—an angle—with the "run" of the cut. Move tool forward in direction of arrow, not sidewise.

With care, the bottom should come off smooth with few if any tool marks. Make sure sides are pared off *before* "bottoming."

Figure 2-2　TO BOTTOM OFF A CARVED SINKING OR SECTION

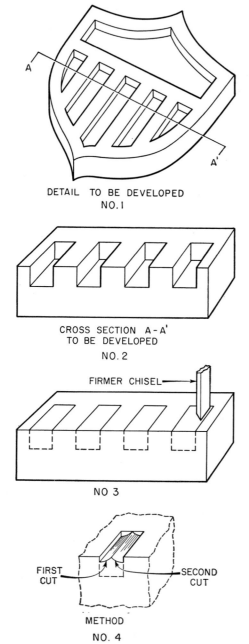

DETAIL TO BE DEVELOPED
NO. 1

CROSS SECTION A - A'
TO BE DEVELOPED
NO. 2

FIRMER CHISEL

NO 3

FIRST CUT

SECOND CUT

METHOD
NO. 4

Figure 2-3 MAKING STOPCUTS

PURPOSE—To Prevent Tools from Overrunning Design

PROCEDURE

1. Hold firmer chisel vertical, bevel *towards* stock to be cut away and *inside* scribed line (No. 3). Mallet chisel down gently to about $\frac{1}{8}$-inch cut. Follow all around inside scribed lines.

2. Remove stock inside chiseled lines, cutting side to side (No. 4) with either firmer or long bent chisel. Continue process to required depth.

3. Bottom off. If curved lines are involved, use properly shaped *straight* gouges to make stopcuts. Cross cut and bottom with *chisels*.

tools are shaped up with a longer lead on the heel than that used for woods of a different character. With this longer lead on the tools, care must be exercised in malleting the tools into the wood to avoid breakage.

White Pine (Photo 7). Our common *Pinus strobus* is a wonderful wood to use for most purposes if you can get wide, clear, heartwood plank. I am not speaking of the pumpkin pine once so common in Maine. I refer to the second growth pine—lumber cut from trees more or less a hundred years old. There are not many of these left; therefore the hunt for this sort of pine is one that may take you far afield. For best results in pine, I emphasize the fact that the stock must be clear. Nothing is more annoying than to have a carving three quarters done and then run into a pitch pocket whose presence in the stock was not foreseen.

If you do have this happen, there are two solutions: one, cut out the pitch pocket and fag in a "dutchman" (see Figure 2-1); the other, throw the carving out the door. White pine lends itself to carvings where the detail is not too small and where long, sweeping modeling cuts are wanted to shade in or develop the larger detail. Care must be taken to see that your tools are always razor sharp. This fact is true for working on any wood, for that matter, but most essential for work on pine. Long cuts are best made with the run of the grain of the wood. Shorter sweeps can be made diagonally across the wood; but directly across the grain, short cuts give better results (Figure 2-2).

In working in pine, care must be taken in driving tools (that is, malleting) to make stopcuts (Figure 2-3); otherwise the stock may split out to the edge of the carving or fracture with the run of the grain. I usually depend upon the strength of my hands and arms to make stopcuts in this wood rather than drive the tools (Photo 3). Pine is best used if the piece can be gessoed (see p. 118) and then either painted or gilded. By using gesso on pine, any errors or small fractures in the detail can be modeled up and it is a further insurance that sap spots will not bleed through the applied finish.

American Walnut (Photo 5). Often called black walnut, this is a hard, dense wood and one that is not too easily carved unless fine, sharp, crisp detail is the major part of the carving. Personally I do not like to use it, although I have done some pieces in the wood and

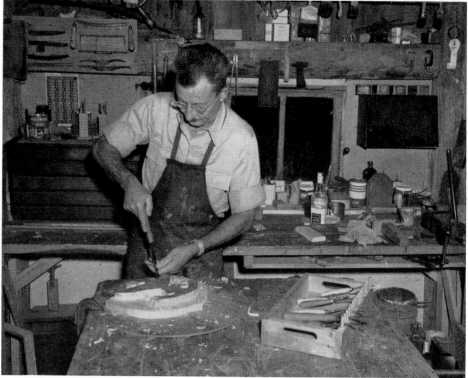

Photo: Flye

Photo 3   Paring off profile of design outline for a stopcut in pine.   (*Courtesy Maine Coast Fisherman*)

the results came up to expectations.   My only objection to walnut is that there is a lot of curl in the grain that sometimes, in fact most frequently, is not visible in the face of the stock when work is started. The tightness of the grain precludes long, sweeping cuts.   No special tool shaping is necessary—sharpness is.

Mahogany.   Mahogany does not grow in this country, and all stock has to be imported from Central America, South America, Africa and the Philippines.   Some experts are of the opinion that African mahogany is not a true mahogany.   I wouldn't know.   I do know that neither Philippine nor African mahogany makes good carving stock when their workability is compared to Amazon or the Central American types.

Amazon mahogany has a slightly softer grain and feel under the carving tools than does Honduras mahogany.   Greater care must be exercised in developing detail with Amazon stock, although it cuts as freely as the other kind. In this mahogany the sharp, clear color differences can be emphasized in the finished piece if the carving is to be oiled and waxed. The color is darker than Honduras mahogany—the grain structure slightly more open.

San Domingo mahogany is without doubt the Crown Prince of fine cabinet woods. Honduras mahogany (Photo 6) is, to my mind, the Crown Prince of wood for carving stock. By preference this is the wood in which I like to work. It cuts freely (Photo 8); there is enough wax in the stock to give slippage to the carving tools; fine crisp detail can be developed; it is strong in cross section; long, sweeping cuts (Photo 9) can be made with the run of the grain, diagonally across the grain, or at right angles to the grain.

With this wood, the finished carving can be oiled and waxed and rubbed up to a fine finish, it can be varnished and rubbed back to a soft glow, it can be left untreated, it can be painted, gilded, or, if you like, thrown out on the ashpile and no harm can come to it. It can be used for out-of-door exposure with no thought for its longevity because it is highly resistant to rot and fungi. It can be dyed, stained, riffled, and abused. You can make mistakes in it, but with reasonable care it can be carved into the most beautiful work the wood carver can produce. I think I am prejudiced in its favor and so my opinion will have to be taken with a grain of salt.

The only trouble with Honduras mahogany is that it is sometimes hard to obtain in the sizes you want for your purpose. Its cost is high. I usually buy two or three plank at a time to have on hand. I ask for kiln-dried stock and, when it comes, I stack it on end in my barn where it can absorb some moisture. I have found that the most convenient and economical sizes for my use are 2-inch thick plank, 14, 16 and 18 inches wide, in lengths of 16 feet. These long lengths can be clipped to the length of the carving blank I want and the width that is best for the particular design or form that I want to execute. If wider blanks are needed, they can be jointed and ripped down to the required width. Save all the short pieces for use, by the way.

When buying any stock for carving blanks, I think it advisable to nave it planed on both sides at the mill. This saves a great deal of time and labor before you start work. Most well-equipped mills cut

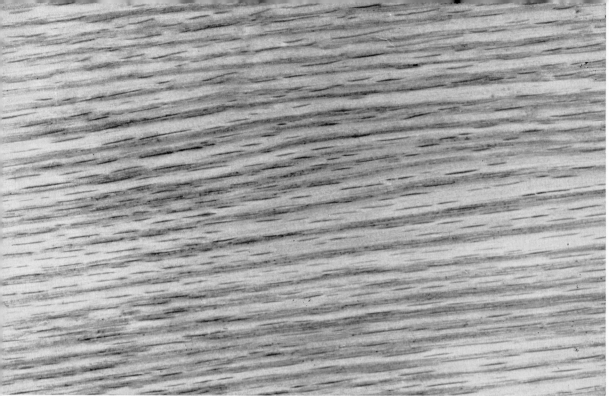

Photo: Flye

Photo 4   Native white oak.   This sample shows the edge grain—note the relative coarse grain structure.

Photo 5   American walnut.   Note tightness of grain structure.

Photo: Flye

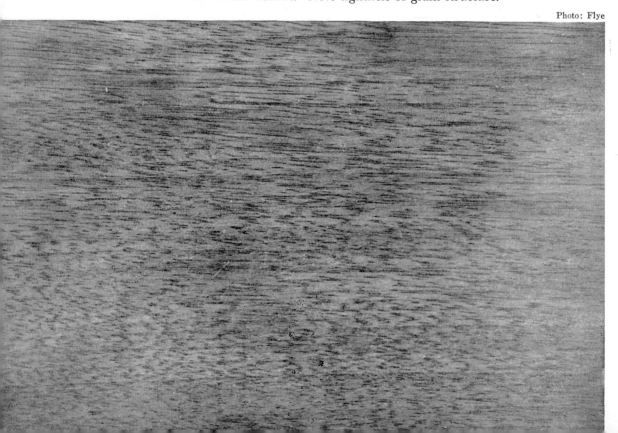

Photo 6   Honduras mahogany.   Note relative openness of grain and lack of "figure" in the wood.

Photo 7   Eastern white pine, *Pinus strobus*.   Heartwood stock slash-sawn.

to the full 2-inch dimension. Common practice calls for $\frac{3}{32}$ inch of stock to be planed off each face. The mill will, if so requested, plane to a full $1\frac{7}{8}$ inch dimension at no extra cost.

In all cases when buying stock I specify that the stock shall be clear, free from shakes and checks; that it shall be kiln-dried and that it shall be protected by coverings to protect the finished faces in shipment. If I am buying from a new source, I also specify that the stock shall be straight-grained. It is advisable to tell the lumber dealer the purpose for which the stock is to be used. He wants to see that you get exactly what you want, and should have—that's his business.

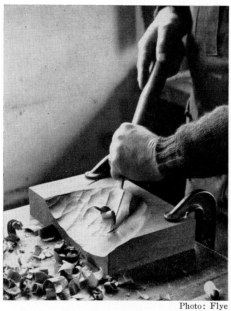 

Photo: Flye   Photo: Flye

Photo 8 (left)   Massive cuts can be made in Honduras mahogany with a long-handled straight gouge. Note the clean cut, no fractures.

Photo 9 (right)   Making a long, sweeping cut in mahogany with the parting tool.

3

The Kind of Tools to Buy and Use

Anyone starting out to buy tools for his shop can go one of two ways. He can buy a lot of tools or he can restrain his impulses and buy tools as he develops the need for them. I suggest that the latter step is the wise one to take, for this reason: the carver's chest can be filled with tools that are used once a year as well as those he uses constantly.

Most companies that sell carver's tools have beginner's sets. Undoubtedly they are the result of long experience on the part of the dealer in selling this sort of equipment and therefore are worth consideration. I have, as I write, the catalogue of "Sculpture Associates" in front of me and in it they have a collection of tools in a set of five. It looks reasonable. It's not expensive, and I think that, to start with, it is adequate. At the end of this chapter, Figures 3-4A and 3-4C show some of the wood carving tools supplied by Sculpture Associates.

All carving tools are sold according to their shape, length, and size. They are classed by the form of the tool; such as "long bend" (or "bent"), "straight," "short bent," "firmer," and "skew." These classifications are further broken down into the following categories: **gouges, chisels, skews,** and **parting tools.** All of these are sold, for the most part, by the actual shape of the cutting edges, which are numbered. Each shape is given an identifying number which is, so far as I know, a standard one. (See Figure 3-4C.)

To clarify this confusion I suggest that you get one of the catalogues from the dealers and study the illustrations. A picture tells the story better than words.

The most useful tools in my chest are shown in Photos 10, 11, 12,

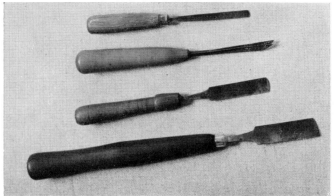

Photo: Flye

Photo 10 I most commonly use these four tools. The long-handled gouge I use for most bosting-out processes. Top to bottom:

⅜-inch #13
  Long Bend Gouge
½-inch #41
  Parting Tool
¾-inch #5
  Straight Gouge
1-inch #4
  Straight Gouge

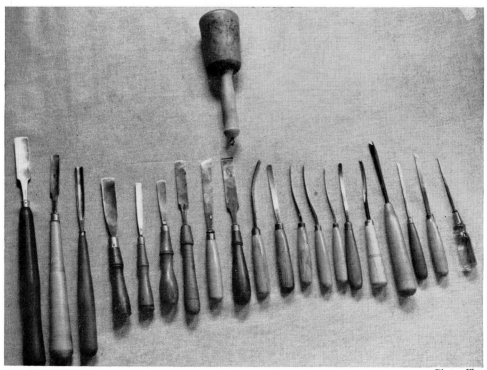

Photo: Flye

Photo 11 Reading from left to right: Top row—Mallet. Second row:

1-inch #4	Straight Gouge		⅜-inch #13	Long Bend Gouge
⅝-inch #5	Straight Gouge		¼-inch #12	Long Bend Chisel
9⁄16-inch #8	Straight Gouge		⅛-inch #12	Long Bend Chisel
1-inch #3	Straight Gouge		¼-inch #12	Long Bend Gouge
7⁄16-inch #5	Straight Gouge		¼-inch #42	Parting Tool
11⁄16-inch #5	Straight Gouge		½-inch #41	Parting Tool
¾-inch #5	Straight Gouge		3⁄16-inch #2	Skew Chisel
¾-inch #2	Skew Chisel		¼-inch #2	Skew Chisel
⅞-inch #1	Firmer Chisel		⅛-inch #1	Spear Chisel
½-inch #15	Long Bend Gouge			

Photo 12 A handful of tools—top to bottom: straight parting tool (note heavy handle), right-hand short bent skew, knife-edged riffler, straight parting tool. (*Courtesy Maine Coast Fisherman*)

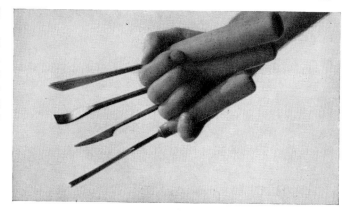

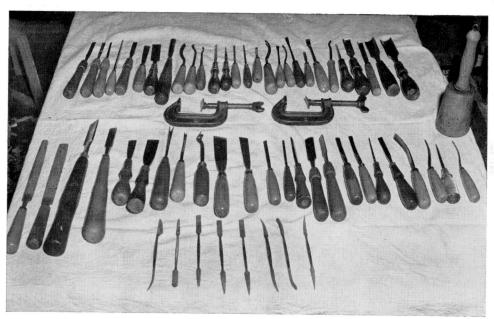

Photo 13 About one half the tools from a carver's chest. These are the tools that are used from time to time. The beginner does not need all these. (*Courtesy Maine Coast Fisherman*)

13. They are identified so that you can see what I think are the most useful, once you get into the serious business of "making something."

The **mallet** is a most important part of the collection. Mine is lignum vitae. It weighs about a pound and a half. That is heavy enough at the day's end to warrant a steak about an inch and a half thick, after you've refreshed the inner man with the cup that cheers. I don't think that a beginner should try a heavier mallet to start with. What the mallet does is to drive the tool in the direction in which it is guided. It can raise a lump on the knuckle of your finger with equal facility. The mallet should be used with caution to begin with. Light, tapping strokes are more effective than hard, driving strokes and a lot less painful if you miss the end of the tool handle—and you will.

By the way, don't try to drive a carving tool with a metal hammer. It isn't a good mallet; it burrs the end of the handle and isn't made for that purpose. Avoid abusing the end of the tool handle because, when you start using the chisel for fine cuts, the end of the handle bears on the palm of your hand and a rough end can raise a blister quickly. I usually varnish all my tool handles when I get them, then rub the varnish off with No. 4 Ought paper and then wax them. This adds protection to the smooth finish and, once done, need not be done again if care is taken in driving the tool.

It is necessary to sharpen all tools after you buy them. They can be rough-sharpened by the dealer when you get them. Even so, you must stone them, hone them, and strop them before you start work. Good **oilstones** can be bought from many sources. I have found that a Carborundum stone with a coarse face and a fine face is a good combination. When I get a new stone I usually soak it in oil. To do this I put the stone in a large-sized tin can such as fruit juices are packed in. Then I fill the can as full as possible with a mixture of light machine oil (automobile oil No. 10) and kerosene—about two parts oil to one of the latter. Let the stone soak a couple of days. Turn it end for end and soak it another day.

This soaking lubricates the stone so that steel chips won't fill the pores of the stone as you use it. A few drops of the same oil on the face of the stone keeps the pores open and floats off the chips. The few drops of oil while you are using the stone prolongs its life, prevents it from getting glazed, and makes it cut faster. All stones other than hones, which are fine-grained natural stones, are better off for this same treatment.

You will need **slips** of various shapes. These are smaller stones—artificial, specially shaped to fit the cutting edges of your tools. They are essential parts of your kit and care should be used to prevent breaking or marring the sharp profiles. Hones should be lubricated with water or saliva.

In sharpening tools, time and care will do a better job than brute strength and awkwardness. Hold the tool on the stone so that the heel of the tool touches the face of the stone in its entirety (Photo 14, Figures 3-1, 3-2). This is important. Nothing is harder to use than a tool on which the heel has been rounded through careless sharpening. I have found that on straight-edged tools—chisels, straight and skew, and parting tools—the best way to bring up an edge is to pass the tool along the oilstone by pushing it forward. Don't try to rotate

Photo: Flye

Photo 14 Position of tool on sharpening stone: in this case, a firmer chisel showing how I hold the tool and flood the stone face with oil.

the tool on the face of the stone until you have become expert at the job. You may round over the corners and that spoils the tool for its designed cut. After the tool has been edged, reverse it and pass the face of the tool—that is, the flat side of a chisel, the reverse side of a skew—across the stone to remove the burr or wire edge. Then hone

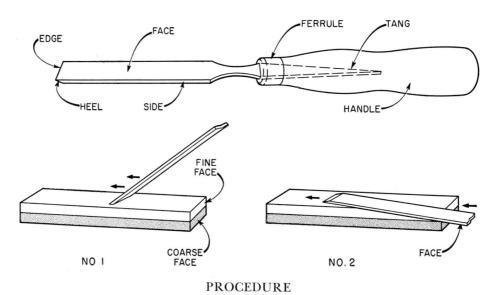

PROCEDURE

1. To sharpen a chisel (or any straight-edged tool), keep heel on stone at angle about 27°. Move tool under light pressure in direction of arrows. Keep edge at approximately right angles to sides of stone.

2. Place face of tool flat on stone. Hold so edge is at slight skew with side of stone. Move with slight pressure on tool in direction of arrows.

Figure 3-1 SHARPENING A CHISEL

the tool on the wet stone the same way. Don't try to hurry the process. There are no short cuts. The finished edge, after honing, should be stropped on leather.

Stropping consists of passing the tool across a leather face. I use a piece of sole leather about 10 inches long, 4 inches wide, with one edge chamfered. Mount this on a 2-inch block, with brads driven into the four corners and *set below the face of the strop*. Load the strop with lapping compound (Carborundum flour, No. 400 grit). Keep the strop moist with oil and, in stropping, put the heel of the tool on the strop and pull toward you. If it is a gouge, rotate the tool from side to side as you pull. Don't push, or you will cut the leather. Use the same procedure on all faces of the cutting edges that can be brought to bear on the leather. Half a dozen strokes ought to be enough if the sharpening and honing have been done properly.

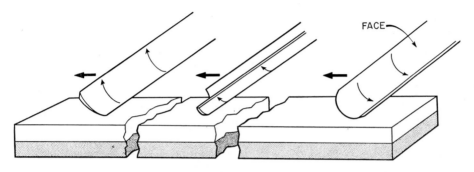

FACE

PROCEDURE

1. Place heel on stone. Move forward, at same time rotating gouge in direction of arrows.

2. Remove wire edge (or burr) with slip. Pull toward handle on inside (face) of gouge. Do not use too much pressure.

Figure 3-2 SHARPENING A GOUGE

By the time you have sharpened your tools you have learned that it isn't the easiest part of the business. Therefore, keep in mind the fact that you don't want to repeat the process. The answer: don't put your tools down on the bench where the fine edge that you've developed can touch any other tool or metal. Don't try to overdrive the tool into hard stock; you'll fracture its edge. I have made a bench tray that I find most useful and I have developed the knack of putting my edged tools back in the tray after I have used them (Photo 15).

Keep the tools in your chest when you don't want to use them. Take out only those tools you think you want for that particular day's work. Don't have too many tools lying about on the top of your bench. If you hit the edge of a tool against another, take time out to resharpen it on the theory that it's nicked. You'll learn; it probably is.

Photo: Flye

Photo 15   Tools in the bench tray.

Never let other people handle your carving tools any more than you would lend them your toothbrush and don't use carving tools for carpentry work.   Buy carpenters' tools.   And vice versa.

Avoid the cutting edges of your tools at all times.   By that I mean never have your hand or arm or body in the direction of the tool's travel.   Don't let anyone stand directly in front of you when you are carving because sometimes the tool slips out of your hand and if, by chance, you are driving the tool, it can go across the shop in a hurry, cutting as it goes.   Never use a carving tool to whittle with.   Use a sharp jackknife.   *Never use a dull tool.*   More accidents are caused by dull tools than sharp ones.   Take care when you use these lethal weapons.   They don't care what they cut, but you do—presumably.

For the sake of argument let's suppose you don't want to buy any machine tools or that you haven't any to start with.   The following hand tools should be acquired:

A **short jack plane,** i.e., an 8-inch plane.

A **jointing plane,** i.e., an 18-inch plane.

A **"turning saw,"** usually called a scroll saw. This is a hard tool to manipulate, but you can use it to advantage, although it will take a lot of practice.

A **hand drill**—the eggbeater type.

A **set of fractional drills,** running from $\frac{1}{16}$ to $\frac{1}{4}$ inch in $\frac{1}{64}$ inch sizes, high speed steel.

A **countersink.**

A **prick punch.**

A **couple of good hand screw drivers.**

A **set of nail sets.**

The best **claw hammer** you can buy.

A **bit brace and four bits,** $\frac{1}{4}$, $\frac{3}{8}$, $\frac{1}{2}$ and $\frac{3}{4}$ inch ought to start you off. If you are going to use plugs and screws for jointed parts, buy,

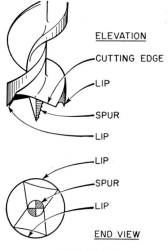

PROCEDURE

1. File off threads on spur on two sides. This prevents threads from dragging tool into wood.

2. File down *outside* of lips a little at a time so that the hole developed in the wood is a press fit for the plug.

Note: If the tool is to be used in drill press, saw off taper on end of shank; if in bit brace, retain this taper end.

Figure 3-3 THE COUNTERBORE. (This tool can be made from stock wood bit.)

as extras, one $\frac{1}{4}$ inch bit, one $\frac{3}{8}$ inch bit. File off the sides of the worm—that is, the threaded portion—on each side so it won't travel into the stock and file down the edges, or the "lips" as they are called; thus, a hole counterbored with the tool will be a press fit for the same-sized plug. (See Figure 3-3.) Two plug cutters, one $\frac{1}{4}$ inch and one $\frac{3}{8}$ inch, can be bought and used in the bit brace for your own use. Take care of the plug cutters because if you have to sharpen them you have to file down the lips of the bit to fit the reduced size.

You also should have:

A good **backsaw,** sometimes called a "tenoning saw."

A good **10-point cross-cut hand saw,** commonly called a "panel saw."

A pair of **carpenter's dividers** and a **carpenter's scribe** (pencil compass).

A good **casemaker's square.**

An accurate **try square** or **combination square** is a "must."

A good wood **straightedge.**

If you are not skilled in the use and application of any of these tools, learn how they are used and why. Handbooks on their use are available. Keep the edged tools sharp and clean from gums and rust.

A **set of rifflers**—specially cut and shaped files—is a necessary part of your carving tool collection.

A **wood rasp.** I find a 10-inch, half round rasp is best.

There are two more tools you can use to advantage, a **spoke shave** and a **draw shave.**

Another point I want to make. Have a place in your shop for everything and keep everything in its place (Photo 16). I'll bet a dollar (Confederate money) you've spent many an hour hunting for a tool you put down somewhere. I know I did before I learned to hang up as many of the carpenter's hand tools on the wall as I could get up.

All these tools can be bought at any good hardware shop or from the "catalogue"—excepting the rifflers which can be bought, usually, from the carving tool dealer.

All the tools I have mentioned have their place in a wood carver's scheme of things, as will be shown. All of them require skill in their proper use, and they can be abused, too. Sharpen edged tools in the list given above in the same manner as is described for carver's tools.

Keep in mind the fact that a lot of strength need not be put forth in using tools of any sort. Let the tool edge do the work; your primary function is to guide the tool in the direction you want it to go and in the manner you want it to cut. It is more advantageous to make a lot of light cuts than a couple of heavy ones. The final results are better, and less effort is required. Also, the tools can be guided better.

Machine tools are timesavers only. They cost money. They will

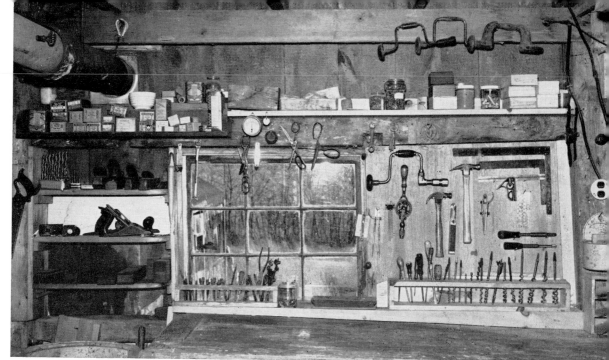

Photo 16 "A place for everything and everything in its place." Part of the wall space taken up with the most generally used carpenter's and casemaker's tools in my shop.

cut anything in front of the blade; fingers (as I know to my sorrow); clothes, if you wear loose, floppy things; wood, metal, and anything else.

The first axiom—never wear loose, floppy garments when you work around machines. Never wear a necktie. Never have the tabs of your shop apron tied in front of you. Don't have loose cuffs on your coveralls. These are mantraps and, if they get caught in the moving blades, will yank you or your hand into the blade and that is that. Keep your hands and fingers away from all machine tools; two inches is the *close limit*.

For machine tools, if you want them, I would suggest a **band saw** (Photo 17). In addition to the band saw, a **table saw** or its equal is good and a great help. A small **drill press** is one of the useful tools that can be had in the shop. You can go on from there and spend lots more, but, in my opinion, you don't have to. Personally, I won't have a rotary jointer in the shop. I dislike this tool and have seen too many accidents resulting from its use even by skilled workmen.

Each of the foregoing machine tools requires some skill in getting the most out of it. I suggest that trial cuts be made in waste stock until you have learned the basic use of each tool.

Photo: Flye

Photo 17 Work on band saw. Note that my hands and fingers are held well
away from the blade. This is important!

Excellent machine tools can be obtained or ordered by mail from
the leading mail-order houses. The best-made tools are legion and
there is a large choice among reputable tool manufacturers. Handbooks are available for each of these tools, usually put out by the maker
or, in the case of the catalogue houses, from them. Read the rules and
abide by them. Safety in the shop is an ESSENTIAL MUST. The
directions for all machine tools will emphasize this point, too.

In the final analysis, don't overbuy tools at the start. Be content
to use the humble tools first. Learn by practice how to sharpen those
that you have, to take care of them, and how to get the most out of them
and how to keep your digits intact.

One final parting shot. Let the tool do the work. Take your
time. Don't hurry. Go easy. Quit when you get tired. Don't work
more than six hours a day on any project and be careful.

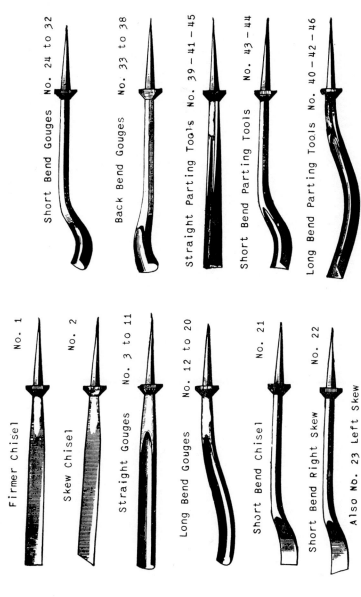

Figure 3-4A   SHAPES AND NAMES OF CARVING TOOLS (*Courtesy Sculpture Associates, 101 St. Mark's Place, New York 9, N. Y.*)

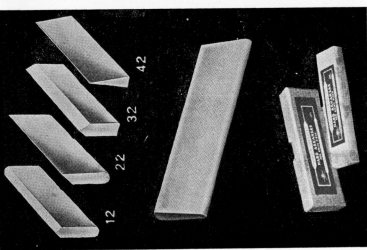

Figure 3·4B   SLIPS AND STONES *(Courtesy Sculpture Associates)*

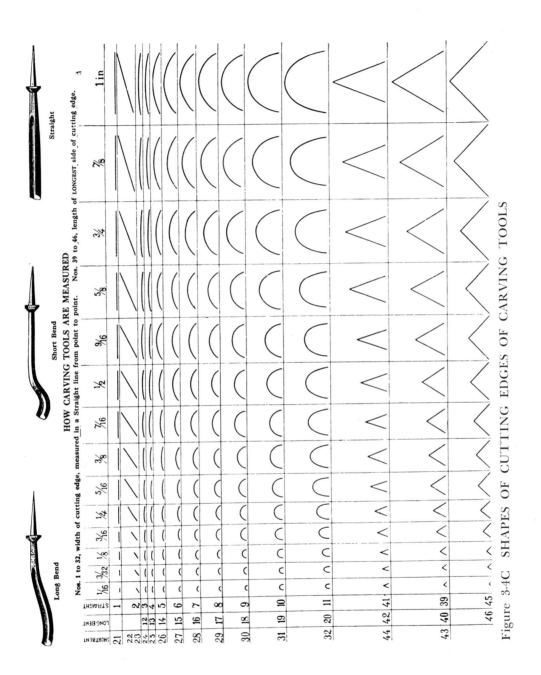

Figure 3-4C SHAPES OF CUTTING EDGES OF CARVING TOOLS

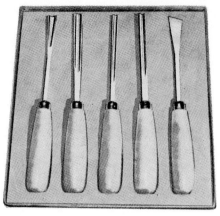

Figure 3-4D BEGINNER'S SET

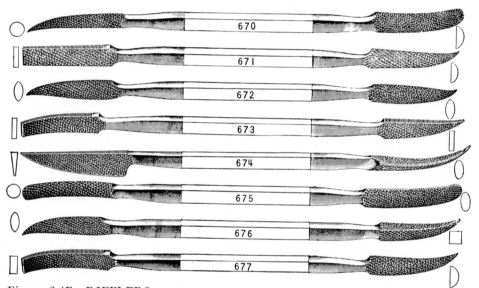

Figure 3-4E RIFFLERS

Figure 3-4F RASP

Figure 3-4G RASP

4

The Wood Carver's Bench and Shop

The important thing to keep in mind in planning your workshop is to have ample space around your carving bench. I find that, for my purposes, a clear space of 30 inches all the way around is ample. This enables me to manipulate any carving about the bench top with no fear that I will hit the walls of the shop or the adjacent benches.

For artificial light I have found that four 150-watt lamps are ample. These are spaced, roughly, above the four corners of the carving bench. For daylight, if it is at all possible, have ample windows on the north side of the shop. This light is diffused and casts thin shadows as you work on the bench. Direct sunlight should be avoided.

The **carving bench** should be fastened firmly to the shop floor. I show a drawing of my bench in Figure 4-2. Note that the bench is braced both ways on each side. This is for stiffening purposes. The size has been ample even for extremely large carvings. The legs are toe-nailed to the floor with eight-penny nails.

The most satisfactory bench top I have found is made up of hemlock plank. These plank are set on the frame with a 3-inch overlap at the ends and 2-inch overlap on the sides. I fasten them to the frame with wood screws set in counter-bored and drilled holes, the counter-bored holes being filled with plugs. In this case the plugs are not glued in place. I like hemlock tops for this reason: the stock holds brads and is soft enough so that if you happen to run a carving tool off the carving and onto the bench top it will shear part of the wood but not harm the tool edge.

I don't bother to do more than smooth the bench top off with the jack plane once in a while. I do not glue the top up either. I have used this carving bench with complete satisfaction for seven years and it is still in good condition.

A cast steel woodworker's screw vise should be fastened to one side of the carving bench (Photo 18). In my case, I face the steel jaws with wooden faces, using either yellow birch or maple for this purpose. My vise jaw faces are 21 inches long, ⅞ inches thick, and about 6 inches wide. I replace them whenever the inside faces get abused, usually every two years.

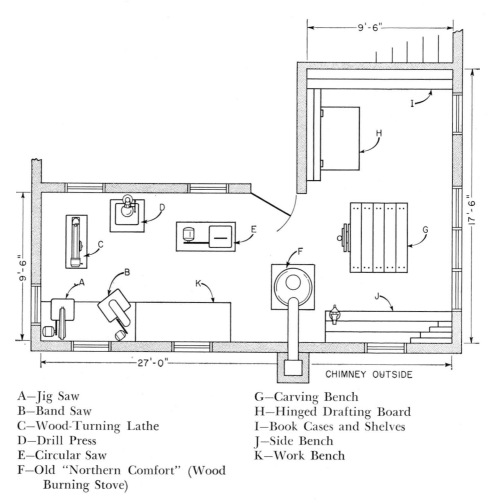

A—Jig Saw   G—Carving Bench
B—Band Saw   H—Hinged Drafting Board
C—Wood-Turning Lathe   I—Book Cases and Shelves
D—Drill Press   J—Side Bench
E—Circular Saw   K—Work Bench
F—Old "Northern Comfort" (Wood
    Burning Stove)

Figure 4-1 PLAN OF WORK SHOP—27 feet long, 9½ feet wide, plus elevation: 9½ feet x 8 feet.

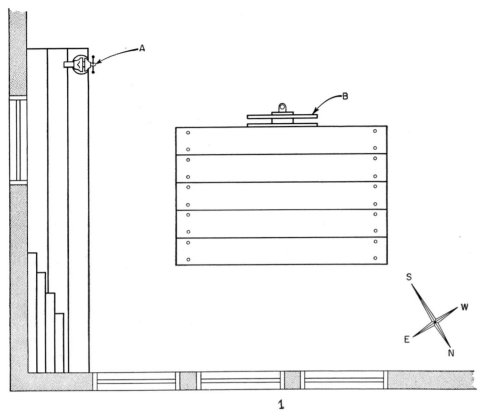

1

Figure 4-2A   PLAN OF SHOP, SHOWING CARVING BENCH, SIDE
BENCH, TOOL RACK, METALWORKING VISE (A), WOODWORK-
ING VISE (B), WINDOWS, ETC.

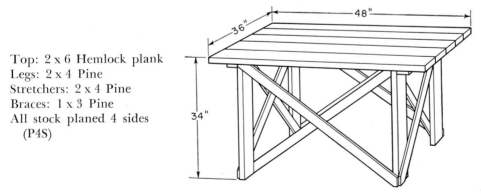

Top: 2 x 6 Hemlock plank
Legs: 2 x 4 Pine
Stretchers: 2 x 4 Pine
Braces: 1 x 3 Pine
All stock planed 4 sides
     (P4S)

Figure 4-2B   ISOMETRIC DRAWING OF CARVING BENCH

Photo: Flye

Photo 18   The woodworker's vise on the carving bench.   Note long, wooden faces on this vise.   Yellow birch can be used for faces.

If the top of your bench does get abused, plane it off to keep the splinters under control.

If you use brads to hold small work in place with edgings, when the latter are removed, pull out the brads with the claw hammer.

I find that a side bench is a most handy adjunct.   Mine is 2 feet wide and 8 feet long.   I keep my carving tool chest on it as well as a miscellany of other things—pencil holders, work gloves, torn sandpaper, paper handkerchiefs, bottles of water, oil and turpentine, sometimes reference data, and generally what-have-you.   It's a handy place for visitors to lean against and sometimes sit upon, too.

The **tool rack** can be almost any kind of a drawered chest or just pieces of 6-inch pine boards (Photo 15).   It doesn't matter.   The important thing is to have it handy.   For years I had a carving tool rack made up of two pieces of boards with narrow separators set between the tools.   Then I found an old "thread case"—a chest with six drawers —and I use that at the present time.   Don't roll tools up in cloth and then try to find them.   This may result in the edges coming in contact and that means more sharpening.

It is important to have a space available for finishing. If you have to use your carving bench top for this purpose, schedule your work so that you can tie up your shop while the finish you put on the carving can set without dust landing on it and so that you don't have to use the carpenter's tools or your carving tools in the shop until the finish is hard. I use the shed of the house for my drafting and finishing room, but I'll probably have to go back to the barn if my better half starts up her antique shop again. If so, I shall use the loft of the barn for these purposes, sealing it off before I do.

Your drawing table can be extemporized from your carving bench, if necessary, by using a piece of ⅝ inch plywood as a drafting table top. If you do, have it clipped absolutely square. I use a piece 30 x 72 inches when I have large sections or carvings to design. If not, I use my old drafting table. Use cellophane tape to hold the corners of the drawing paper down if you use plywood. Be sure the plywood top is smooth. The best way to assure this is to dampen the plywood with a moist cloth which raises the grain slightly, then sand it smooth with No. ½ paper, then varnish it, then sand it down again.

You don't need an elaborate set of drafting tools. A tee square and a sharp pencil are good starters. Everyone has an idea as to what a good set of drawing equipment is. Mine are pretty well abused after thirty years of use; some of them are missing; my grandsons use them for their "things." I use them as little as possible. For pencils, I buy a dozen at a time. My wife uses half a dozen of them for her crossword puzzles. The rest I keep sharp and handy to the drafting board. I use three grades: Number Ones for outline drawings, Number Threes for heavy outlines after the sketch is done, and a layout pencil for final shading and definition.

There is a saying in this business, "If you can draw it, you can carve it; if you can't, you can't."

5

Preparation of the Drawing for a Carving

It is reasonable to assume that anyone starting to make a wood carving for the first time will begin with a simple design—one that you feel reasonably sure you can execute. I would suggest that, until you have made several carvings in bas-relief, you should not undertake the more ambitious forms of alto-relievo or of compound carvings.

Photo: Flye

Photo 19 Detail of bookcase showing scallop shell carved intaglio. (*Courtesy Mrs. Glenn Stewart*)

Photo: Flye

Photo 20   Corner cupboard carved in bas relief and alto-relievo. Owned by the
Author.

There are four forms of relief carving. The conventional terms are:

Intaglio. The carving is done so that all detail is worked out below the surrounding surfaces—in other words, hollowed out (Photo 19).

Cameo. Most frequently termed *bas-relief* (Photos 20 and 52). In this form the design is raised very slightly above the surrounding surfaces. The modeling is very sharply defined, but the form is developed more in the way that the design is drawn than in the height of the modeled planes.

Mezzo-Relievo. This term is applied to a carving where the modeled planes are elevated to some degree above the surrounding surfaces and the final effect is developed in the modeling of the design rather than in the drawn perspective, as in the case of *bas-relief.*

Alto-Relievo (Photos 20 and 54). In this form the detail is boldly developed in every plane above the surrounding surfaces. The contrasts between the various planes of the carving are sharply delineated.

To fix in your mind the sort of carving you want to make, it is necessary to put it down on paper. A series of preliminary studies of the project will illustrate the difficulties ahead. It may be of help if I outline briefly the steps I take to commit the new carving to paper before I execute it in wood.

For drawing in the preliminary details I use old-fashioned brown wrapping paper for my layout sheet. I do this because it is inexpensive, it takes pencil lines well, it is finished hard enough to stand erasures, and it can be used for shading in. You can throw it away with no regrets. I get a 24-inch wide roll weighing about 60 pounds for something like $6.00 and it lasts a couple of years. Beside which, you can wrap parcels up in it.

After a little practice, I find I can make a preliminary sketch almost to full scale, free hand. I call these layout sketches (which may not be the term used by the cognoscenti, but it will do). I start these layout sketches by drawing in the head of an eagle (assuming I am working out a new design for an eagle) in a corner of the paper. Then somewhere else I lay out a section of the wing detail, then somewhere else on the paper I sketch in the pose and usually draw out various variations of these details. By so doing, I fix in my mind many of the details I want to develop in the final design. Usually these sketches will have covered most of the sheet. Starting afresh, I lay out a "box" (or

Photo: Flye

Photo 21 Detail of bookcase cornice and valance board showing application of rope molding and associated parts. (All these moldings were carved by hand.) Detail of scallop shell carved alto-relievo. (*Courtesy Mrs. Glenn Stewart, South Bristol, Maine*)

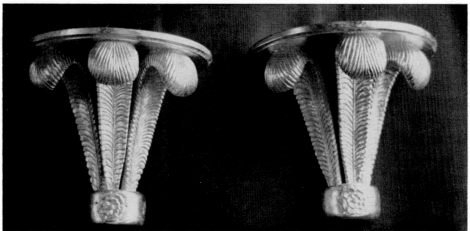

Photo: Upton

Photo 22 Pair wall brackets carved in full round using Prince of Wales plumes as supporters with the Tudor Rose on the base. (*Courtesy Mrs. Glenn Stewart, South Bristol, Maine*)

rectangle, if you prefer) the length and width of the carving I am to draw.

The box is drawn exactly to the dimensions of the carving. The next step is to draw in centerlines in both directions. The point of their intersection is the exact center of the box. Using these center-lines as reference points, I draw in all the details that are shown in the layout sketches.

For the sake of illustration and simplicity the major part of the eagle will be alike on both sides. Usually I draw in the head first, then the outline of the left wing, then the outline of the tail and the bottom rest. All this is only one half of the eagle.

The next step is to trace off the outline on thin, transparent trac-ing paper; indexing * the center intersection of the vertical and hori-zontal lines and the upper and lower corners of the box. Then I re-verse the tracing paper in such a manner that these indexed points coincide with the ones on the working drawing. Backing the tracing paper up with carbon paper, I trace over the outline. The corners of the tracing paper are, of course, fastened down to the drawing board. I check to see that I have gone over all the outline. If I have skipped any part of it, I retrace.

The next step, I remove the tracing paper and view the completed outline. Frequently it will be evident that the whole outline is not ex-actly what I want. The sweep of the wings may be altogether too greatly exaggerated or the tail outline is too wide or too narrow or out of proportion to the rest of the carving. In other words, I've pulled a "bubu."

Correcting these out-of-drawing errors by erasing the faulty parts, I revise one side and retrace until the outline is just as I want it to be. Then, and only then, do I start lining out the drawing with the de-tail. I usually draw in the feet in the position I want them on the bottom rest. Then I draw out the legs with the feathering indicated, then I draw in the detail of the head, the beak, the cere, eye, nostril and crest. The body and wing feathers are only indicated for the rea-son I know perfectly well that when I come to this part of the carving I will have thought of a new way in which I want to execute these essential details.

---

* Indexing is simply marking register points on both the tracing paper and the drawing so that you can always overlap the tracing exactly in the same place on the drawing whenever you need to.

Photo: Upton

Photo 23 A small American Eagle showing the various parts assembled after being profiled, jointed and bosted out. The completed eagle is shown in the next photograph. A compound carving.

Photo: Flye

Photo 24 A small American Eagle. Dimensions—Wing to wing 24 inches; height, 22 inches; overall length, 24 inches; gilded; eyes colored. (*Courtesy Mrs. Glenn Stewart, South Bristol, Maine*)

Often it is a great help to make additional drawings such as cross sections, both in the vertical plane and the horizontal plane, using the centerlines as the reference points for these sections. If the carving is to be done in "alto-relievo," I sometimes shade in various portions of the plan—that is, the layout drawing—to show to what degree the detail is to be raised and what the final carving is supposed to look like.

These drawings are the final preparatory steps. The working drawings are made from tracings of the completed layouts.

The reason for all this preliminary work is to be sure that your idea is developed as you see it in your mind's eye. If the drawing is not as you want it to be, if you don't like the way it looks, if it does not portray the picture you have in mind, by all means throw it away and start anew. I have often made half a dozen drawings of a new pose or new form of eagle before I was satisfied with the over-all picture.

It is always easier to correct your mistakes with a pencil on paper than with a carving tool on the carving block. The care and patience with which you make your layout sketches are reflected in the finally executed carving.

When I make my drawings I try to keep a picture of how I am going to make out of wood the parts I have drawn. It is quite essential that this be kept in mind. There are certain limitations to what can be done with wood. I cannot, within the compass of this work, begin to enumerate them. They have to be found out through experience.

Before you commit your drawing to the carving block, or to limbo as the case may be, walk off and take a long look at it. Then walk out the door. Forget it. Go about some other business for half a day. Take up your mind with other things. This is quite important. After you come back and review the drawing, you will, in all probability, see where it can be improved. Make the evident or obvious changes then and there. Oftentimes a coffee break at this juncture is a lot of help. A few minutes spent in studying your design will show you the difficulties you may have to overcome in the actual carving.

Never let these difficulties deter you from proceeding with the work. Go ahead. If you make mistakes, keep this in mind: you can always start over again. "The man who never does anything always has the eraser on his pencil unused." All my pencils are well worn down at the eraser end.

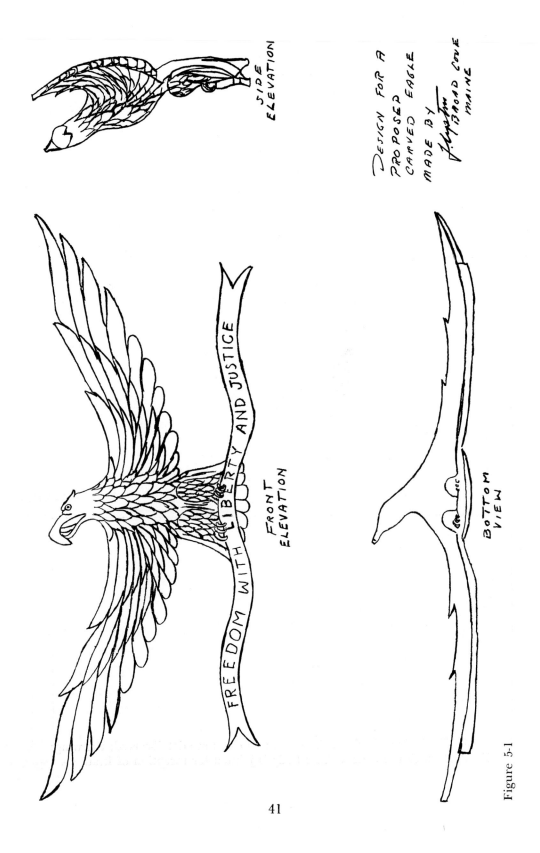

SIDE ELEVATION

DESIGN FOR A PROPOSED CARVED EAGLE

MADE BY *Knowlton* BROAD COVE MAINE

FRONT ELEVATION

FREEDOM WITH LIBERTY AND JUSTICE

BOTTOM VIEW

41

Figure 5-1

Photo 25 This and the next four photographs show the processes followed in building up, bosting and detailing the elements for a Bremen Eagle. In this illustration the wings and head are profiled and bosted out. (*Courtesy Malden National Bank, Malden, Massachusetts. Gift of Mr. Harry F. Damon of Tamworth, New Hampshire*)

Photo 26 The body and wings. The legs and claws are detail-carved; the wings lined out with the pencil. The body is jointed for reception of head.

Photo 27   The head and body pad detail-carved.

Photo 28   The elements are assembled.   All detail carving is done.   The final step will be to polychrome the carving.

Photo 29   The completed carving.   This eagle measures 48 inches wing tip to wing tip, 17 inches high, with the head projecting 9½ inches.

Keep in mind the fact that, as you work with wood, as your carving grows from a piece of plank to the final piece, you will see places where you think it would be improved by departing from your design. If that is so, make the changes forthwith. After all, it is your design, your carving, your idea—and if you can't change your mind, well, why say more?

Once you are completely satisfied with your original layout in all respects, it may be of some help to make a projection of the drawing so that you can see all the varying planes you want to develop on paper. These can be done by shading in or by making a series of isometric drawings, as the case may be. These are only aids and should not be followed in the final work.

If you have progressed from a bas-relief to an alto-relievo you may well want to undertake a more difficult piece of work. An illustration of this project is shown in Photos 25–29. This Bremen Eagle has a projecting head, a body pad, and the base plane of the wings. It is built up by joining the various pieces with glue and wood screws and plugs. All of these steps will be covered in Chapter 6.

The drawings for this sort of work are more difficult to do than is the case where the carving is to be more or less in one plane. Each of the parts will have to be drawn to full scale before they are put together in your layout drawing. I make these full-sized drawings on the same paper as that which I use for the layout, using layout or guide lines in the same manner as I do those in the final layout so that the various parts can be traced over in their proper positions. This enables me to vary the position of the head at will. I may want to increase or decrease the angle of the head. In some positions the head will seem to be more alert than in other positions, or perhaps more aggressive, or even less so.

Each part of a compound carving such as this must be made separately. Keep in mind how the grain of the wood is to run in each piece; what the mechanical difficulties are going to be in the preparation of each piece; how the various pieces are going to be joined; how they are going to be finished carved with the detail shown on the drawing.

I point out all these things for the reason that it is easier to think the problem out on paper than it is to get the parts out wrong. I have in my shop a couple of carvings I have never finished, as reminders that I undertook a piece of work that I had not thought out thoroughly on paper at the beginning. They are lugubrious reminders that I can be optimistic about my capacity.

The working drawing—that is, the one you take to the carving bench with you—can be either the layout drawing or a series of tracings from this drawing. It should be of such character that it can be placed on the carving block and transferred thereto by tracing off the outlines. Backing up the working drawing with carbon paper—the carbon side face down on the block—go over the entire outline and the places where stopcuts are to be made. Here is where you see why it is advantageous to have your carving stock planed by the mill before-

Photos 30 and 31 "Some people want angels." This illustrates a carving in the round about which I had some doubts until I committed it to the carving block. (*Courtesy Rev. G. Ernest Lynch, Rector, Trinity Church, Indianapolis, Indiana*)

Bull's-eye mirror frame and eagle. This compound carving is made up of 3 parts for the eagle and 6 parts for the frame. (*Courtesy W. D. Thompson, Jr., Concord, New Hampshire*)

 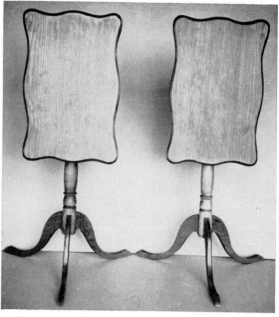

Photos 32 and 33 Caduceus carved in alto-relievo, polychromed staff, gilded serpent, oiled and waxed background. (*Courtesy Drs. Roland and Mary Price, Armour, South Dakota*)

"Some people want tables." A pair of candlestands—pine tops, maple columns and feet. (*Courtesy Mrs. Carl R. Frye, Columbus, Ohio*)

hand. Any obvious blemishes on the stock will show through the tracing paper and the drawing can be shifted to avoid them.

When you have a compound carving drawn up that you want to do, have all the tracings for the various parts at hand. Lay out each part on the carving blank. Arrange the several drawings in such manner that they are separated from an adjacent drawing by at least an inch. Be sure that the drawings are laid out so that the run of the grain of the wood is similar in all pieces. Do not try to crowd the drawings together. Be sure that a separating cut on one part does not intersect another part. Keep in mind that you will have to saw out these various parts on the band saw or with the scroll saw. Be sure this can be done. The only reason for doing this, laying out the components, is to be sure that the same characteristics of the wood will be similar in all pieces. This makes it easier to proceed with the carving.

6

Getting Out the Parts and Gluing

In getting out sailing orders for vessels that are to make a sea voyage there is a sentence that goes: "Being in all respects ready for sea—" that I should like to paraphrase into: "Being in all respects ready to go to work." You are about ready to start the hard business of getting out the part or parts of your carving. The necessary transfers to the carving block have been done. I have found it very helpful to go over the carbon lines on the blank with a soft pencil, darkening them so that the lines stand out prominently. It helps tremendously to be able to see the lines when you saw out along the profile lines.

Care must be taken to saw along these lines on the waste stock side. After some practice, you will find that you can follow along the outside of the marks if you do not try to hurry. You should also be careful not to cut into the face of the carving with the saw. I try to keep in mind the fact that the profile of the carving is just as important to the overall picture as is the detail. The profile sets the outside limits to your work and, if these limits are irregular (assuming you don't want them that way, that is), the whole piece is thrown out of balance.

The profile can be done on the band saw or with the scroll saw. If the scroll saw is used, great care should be taken to see that the saw is held at right angles to the face of the stock and that the blade does not veer from the vertical as you saw. If you are a new hand at the business, try a lot of cuts in waste stock until you have learned how to handle this difficult tool. I am frank to admit that I still find the scroll saw one of the trickiest things to use properly that I know of. But skill can be acquired in its use, just the same.

For profiling out 2-inch stock on the band saw where there are a number of sharp angles or small-radius curves involved, I find that using a ⅛-inch wide band-saw blade works best. For longer sections or more or less straight line cuts or on large-radius curves, I use a ¼-inch blade. Here, let me emphasize the fact that it is the saw that must do the work. Don't try to crowd the work into the saw; keep it moving at a slow steady pace with just enough pressure on the piece to keep new stock in contact with the blade (Photo 17).

Never take the guard off the band saw. Never get your fingers within two inches of the moving blade. Never try to clear the saw of a bit of stock if it gets jammed when the saw blade is in motion. Stop the tool. Keep your mind on the work at hand ALL the time. I speak from bitter experience. I nearly lost the end of my finger on that mantrap simply because I became absent-minded and thought more about how I was going to get the carving made than how I was doing on the saw. Not only did I lose a lot of time, but, in addition, I went through quite a lot of discomfort. And all this after some thirty years of being around and running many kinds of machines, too.

The band saw blade moves in one direction constantly—downwardly. I was in a man's shop several years ago who had just set up a new band saw and he was trying to make it work. He got nowhere and the shop was filled with smoke and bad language. He had the saw in upside-down. It's easy to do, if you don't watch yourself. Manuals are available on the proper use of this tool from various sources. Used properly it is a great help.

To follow various curved lines on the band saw the work is rotated about the saw blade. This is done by using both hands on the stock and swinging or rotating the stock about on the table. It is not a difficult procedure, once it is tried.

The jigsaw (Photo 34), which I have not mentioned before (forgot it, I guess), can be used for profiling out carvings if the stock is not too thick. I sometimes use my jigsaw on 2-inch stock, but it's slow work and considerable care must be taken in feeding stock to the blade to see that you don't break the thin saw. On 1-inch stock it is very good. All sharp turns can be made readily. The advantages of the jigsaw are that it costs somewhat less than the band saw to begin with; also, it is a more versatile tool in that interior cuts for pierced work can be made on it, as well as exterior cuts. The blades cost a

Photo: Flye

Photo 34 Cutting out for a piercing on the jigsaw. To start, the saw blade is disconnected from driving arm and head chuck, led up through the bored holes and re-chucked; then the stock is manipulated about the saw blade along the profile lines.

lot less than band saw blades so that if you break them your heart need not bleed.

No matter which of these three types of saws are used to profile the carving, best results come from the degree of care with which you manipulate the stock about the saw or, in the case of the scroll saw, the saw about the work.

If you take time to follow the darkened outline, the result will be that you have less edge finishing to do on the piece after it is cut.

In the event that your design calls for two pieces to be jointed together to develop the proper thickness, the following suggestions may be of help. Lay out one profile on the stock, being sure that the design does not overlap the edge. Have on hand a duplicate piece of stock the same size as the first one. Using the jack plane, joint both faces to be joined so that the grain in both pieces runs the same way. Do not glue together at this point; wait. Profile out one piece, either with the power tools or with the scroll saw, being sure you stay outside the lines. Place the profiled piece on top of the other one, jointed faces together, and trace around the first piece, then cut carefully about the lines on the second piece. It will be a trifle larger than the first one. Then glue and clamp both pieces of profiled stock together. When the glue has set—usually overnight—pare off the sides of the larger piece to fit the top piece. Then you are ready to pare off both pieces to the exact profile you want to develop.

The procedures outlined above hold true for any step in the carving where two or more thicknesses of stock are required to develop a given part.

Built-up sections of the carving that are all within its periphery are jointed together in somewhat different manner. The steps that I follow in this instance are these:

Joint the face of that portion of the carving that will form the base.

Joint the piece that is to be applied to the base stock, after it has been roughly outlined and sawed or planed to the desired thickness.

Drill and countersink the necessary holes so that the two pieces of stock can be held in place while they are bosted out; then bost out.* Index the overlay (the second piece of stock) at two points, remove the wood screws, apply glue, replace the screws and draw the two pieces together as tightly as possible with the screws. Use additional clamps if necessary to be sure that equal pressure is applied throughout the joint. This is best determined by the fact that, if in applying glue to both faces in equal amounts and having it spread about in equal quantity, about the same amount of glue will be squeezed out at the edges of the pieces.

A tip about placing holes—be sure that the screw holes do not come close to the edges where you may hit them with the carving tools. If you want to make doubly sure that you will never hit a metal screw with the carving tools: counter-bore the holes so that, regardless of the thickness of the stock, the shank of the screw (the unthreaded portion of the wood screw below the head) is left in the overlay.

Be sure that, when you drill the holes in the overlay, the holes in the base coincide with them. You can fill the counter-bored holes with as many plugs as necessary to bring the top of the top plug up to the face of the overlay or use long plugs; either way is satisfactory.

This fact must be kept in mind always. You cannot joint two

---

* Bosting is the technical term for making the rough cuts, or rough carving. Its purpose is to eliminate all the surplus wood from the face of the piece.

pieces of stock together using the mill-planed faces. You must hand-plane each piece to a perfect fit before you can be sure that the joints will take glue and hold together properly.

Jointing is the art of planing parts to make each piece perfectly smooth and flat so that, when two pieces are put together, they fit with

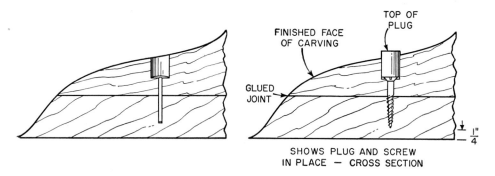

SHOWS PLUG AND SCREW
IN PLACE — CROSS SECTION

PROCEDURE

Drill hole in both pieces of stock, after clamping them together. Hole should be smaller than root of wood screw thread below shank. Drill to about ¼ inch of bottom of bottom piece of stock (*left*).

Use counterbore for plug hole (same size, of course). Counterbore ½ inch deep in drilled hole. Note: Always index stock across both pieces by pencil marks for re-assembly of pieces.

Unclamp stock. Glue both faces. Assemble. Run wood screw home with screw driver tight enough to draw stock together. Wipe bottom end of plug with glue and put some on lower edges. Place in hole over screw and tap home. Let glue set and pare off top of plug. Be sure grain of plug and stock run the same way—*always* (*right*).

Figure 6-1 TO SET A PLUG

no high or low spots. For face jointing—that is, planing the flat sides of two pieces to be jointed—set the blade of the plane fine. On the faces of the pieces that are to be joined by glue, take off very thin curls; start planing across the grain, then lengthwise with the run of the grain. Keep at it on both pieces until you get as perfect a fit as you can. Don't forget that a lot of fine cuts are better than a few coarse cuts and far easier to do.

If you are going to joint two sides of stock edgewise, care must be

Photo: Flye

Photo 35 Jointing the edge of a 2-inch mahogany plank. Note the slight skew the jointer plane makes with the stock. Set the plane blade fine for this process.

taken to see that both sides are planed flat, square, and straight. This is best done with the 18-inch jointer plane (Photo 35). It will take a considerable amount of practice to be able to do this. A good edge joint is one where both edges are perfectly square with the face of the stock, where the ends touch each other for about two-thirds of the length of the pieces and where there is a thin gap in the center of the joint when the two pieces are placed one on the other vertically— the gap in the center being about the thickness of a cigarette paper— no more.

To glue two pieces of stock together edgewise, it is necessary to use long clamps. Specially designed fixtures are available today that fit on short or long pieces of galvanized iron pipe. These pairs of devices, together with a suitable length of pipe, make excellent clamps for shop use.

There is a trick in setting your clamps on the stock to get the best results. On any longitudinal joint up to 4 feet, I have found that the best results are obtained by setting the clamps in from each end a distance of 8 or 9 inches. Clamps so placed will pull all parts of the joint tightly together, and there is enough spring in the stock so that the narrow gap in the center of the joint will be drawn up tightly.

To avoid crushing the edge grain of your carving blank, put a small piece of stock (I use clipped ends of untempered Prestwood for the purpose) between the inside faces of the jaws of the clamps and the edges of the stock (Photo 36). To prevent the stock from twisting or curling out of the clamps, I usually use small hand clamps set over the joint at either end of the piece. To be sure that the clamps are not glued to the wood, put squares of paper over the joints, back these up with the Prestwood clips, "put the squeeze on," and you are sure that the two pieces will stay put. Another thing that may be useful to do is to slip pieces of newspaper in between the pipe and the glued joint. This avoids the possibility of the stock becoming glued to the pipe after the glue is set. Do not be afraid to squeeze the two pieces of stock tightly together. The tighter the clamps, the better the result.

If you have made your joints square and a good fit, the amount of glue that is squeezed out from the joint after you have set up the pipe clamp should be about the same all along the joint on both sides.

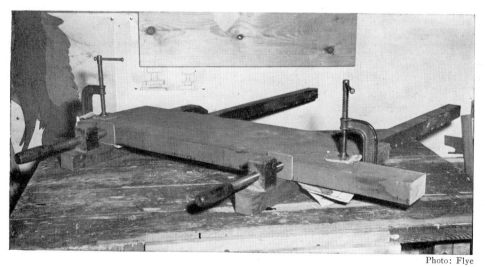

Photo: Flye

Photo 36 Stock in clamps after jointing and gluing up. Note the clipped stock between the plank and the various clamps, also the bits of paper. The "C" clamps prevent the stock from curling out of the large ones.

One tip about reglueing a piece if you have to, for some reason or another. Always wash off, with very hot water, all the glue that has been applied. Set the pieces aside to dry thoroughly and, after they have dried, correct the error of fit or whatever it is that must be done. Then follow out the glueing and clamping procedures as before. Don't try to work wet or damp stock. Anything you do under these conditions will be distorted when the stock dries. Wood always swells out of line when wet or damp.

I have used a number of different glues. The old-fashioned hot glue is messy, hard to work, and is not water resisting. The best glue that I have used so far is Weldwood water-resisting glue. It was, perhaps at one time, called waterproof glue. I am frank to confess that I have not used the presently available instant-set contact glue. Whether it's because I am of the school that believes that two glued faces should be rotated about one another to get a good spread or that I am old-fashioned, I wouldn't know. Both, maybe. Be that as it may, some of my carvings have been in the weather for eight years and they are still in one piece so far as I know.

It well may be that I am harping on one string too long, but—again I want to emphasize—don't try to hurry work along. Plan the various steps so that you don't have to rush to get the work done. By that I don't mean that you should sit on your hands and do a lot of wishful thinking, either.

7

Bosting Out, or Rough Carving

I have found that the best way to hold a carving in place on the work bench is to fasten the back of the profiled blank to a piece of quarter-inch hardwood plywood. I stumbled on this scheme after using several different means to secure the piece. I would suggest a round piece, about 18 inches in diameter, laid out in pie-shaped sections by pencil and having holes drilled and countersunk at regular intervals along the pencilled lines as shown in Figure 7-1.

I fasten this plywood to the back of the carving with three screws, usually ¾ inch, No. 8 in size. Curiously enough, these three wood screws have never failed to hold the carving in place, no matter how much I work on the design. By having the plywood hold-down overlap the edges of the profiled piece, you have room to clamp the plywood to the edge of the bench with steel or cast iron clamps. Nomi-

I use ⅝-inch or ¾-inch #8 steel wood screws to attach this hold-down to the back of the carving. Usually 3 screws are enough. Suggested diameter—18 inches, using ¼-inch hardwood plywood.

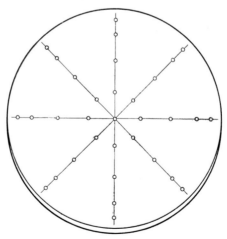

Figure 7-1 PLAN OF THE HOLD-DOWN (OR BACK-UP) USED TO CLAMP FLAT CARVINGS DOWN TO THE BENCH

nally I clamp the whole business to a corner. This lets me work on two sides of the piece at will. I seldom remove the carving from the back-up until I have the bosting completed.

The technical term for making the rough cuts is "bosting."

The purpose of bosting out a carving is to eliminate all the surplus wood from the face of the piece. This process is best done with the larger gouges and chisels. The first step in the process is to outline all the detail that is later to be carved or modeled with the smaller tools by making the stopcuts. This is shown in Photos 3 and 74.

These stopcuts are made so that stock will not be removed from the high detail they outline. To make these cuts use variously shaped tools that approximate the outline of the detail that is to remain for further working. I prefer not to use any but straight tools—that is, I find that the long, bent gouges are not suitable for this business of stopcutting; there is too much spring in the tool to drive properly and there is also the danger that you will break the tool. Which I have done when I first started carving.

Reasonable care must be taken in bosting out to the stopcuts after the stock has been removed for the first quarter inch (Photo 37). Prior to that time, chisel out along the stopcuts carefully on the waste stock side.

The purpose of bosting out is to develop the internal planes of the carving to a close approximation of the finished piece. Heavy cuts can be made at first, but as you approach the final surface of these planes, lighter and lighter cuts should be made until you have taken enough stock away so that the form is very close to that you show in the drawings. At this point you will realize why I stressed the necessity of fixing the detail in your mind by careful consideration of all the aspects of the drawing and the form that you want to develop. Somehow or another, you know when you have gone far enough. With a little practice you will find that you seldom overcut your carving.

When you have one side of the design bosted out, proceed with the other. They will be more or less alike if the same process you followed in making the original cuts are duplicated. A great help in this process is to set the low points on the sides of the piece. I do this by using the scribe, measuring each point or reference spot from

Photo: Flye

Photo 37   Bosting out to stopcut.   (*Courtesy Maine Coast Fisherman*)

the surface of the hold-down to the low points of the carving as they
are to show on the sides of the profiled piece and transferring these
low points to the corresponding positions on the other side.   Then
bost out the stock to those markings.

   If it happens that there is a difference in the design for the carving on either side (as in the case of the picture shown in Photo 50),
but there are points where the same amount of stock is to be bosted
out on each side, use the straightedge placed across the areas concerned and measure down from the bottom of the straightedge to
the surface of the bosted section.   Then measure down from the bottom of the straightedge to the corresponding section on the other
side.   The difference in the depths will be shown, and these differ-

Photo: Flye

Photo 38 Starting the back cuts.

ences can then be corrected.   If, as sometimes happens, you have removed too much stock on one side, the differences in depths will have
to be reconciled by removing stock on the side of the carving that is
higher than the other.

This process of bosting out should be done on all parts of the
carving that can be reached conveniently while the blank is fastened
to the hold-down.

Do not attempt, at this time, to do any detailed carving.   You
may have to remove the blank from the bench and the hold-down so
that you can back-cut the reverse side.   Back-cutting (as its name implies) is cutting away stock from the back of the carving (Photo 38).
This is done, in many instances, so that the profile can be finished in
such manner as to give the effect of a third dimension.   It might be
called an exaggerated chamfering process.   If finished detailed work
is done before the back-cutting is undertaken, the probability is that
it will be damaged.

There are many cases, of course, where back-cutting is not to be
done—where the straight or vertical edge of the carving will add to

the final appearance of the piece. This fact you will have to decide for yourself.

In the case of a large and intricate compound carving, all the various pieces will have to be bosted out before any detailed work is undertaken. In the construction of the large American Eagle that is shown in one of the illustrations, each piece was profiled, bosted, jointed, drilled, counter-bored and screwed before any detail carving was undertaken. The purpose of this was to be sure that the planes of each side—the wings, the body, the claws, and the base block—were as nearly alike as it was possible to make them (Photo 39).

When all the parts of this eagle were assembled, the differences became apparent and they had to be reconciled. In all the many pieces that were involved, I had to take reasonable care to see that I did not overcarve. As there was a pair of these eagles, it meant that each piece on each eagle had to be reconciled with the corresponding one. It sounds intricate, involved, and difficult. It wasn't,

Photo 39 Parts for one of a pair of large American Eagles. Note that the base block with claws and legs and the wing surfaces are detail-carved, but no detail carving is done on body section. This should be done after all parts are assembled so that the detail carving on the body will run with the detail carving on the other sections.

really, because I knew beforehand that this would have to be done, and I provided for this contingency as I went along with the work.

Had I not anticipated this, the work would have been much more difficult to execute. And speaking about these eagles, it may not be out of place to tell how they came about.

About the middle of May, 1954, I had a telephone call from a man in Waldoboro who wanted to come down to the shop if I was going to be here. I asked him along. About twenty minutes later a big, tall, heavy-set, good-looking man came in and introduced himself as George Hand.

I couldn't see the connection between his company and my work but I am always willing to learn. So we started to talk. I was working on a rather complicated carving at the time and he began to ask me a lot of questions about my work: how long it took me to make a carving, what I charged for my things, and all sorts of stuff.

We had gotten to the point where he wanted to know if I was tooled up to carve a pair of big American Eagles. I showed him what tools I had and what they could do. I gave him some idea about what I charged for my work and why. About this time, "Jake" Day came in. "Jake," Maurice Day, is the feller who draws all the amusing

Photo 40   The pair of 4-foot American Eagles completed and gilded. (*Courtesy Portland Press Herald—Evening Express*)

Photo: Flye

When bigger EAGLES are made
UPTON will make em!

Photo 41 "No Comment."

animal pictures, full of delightful whimsey. He is also a most gifted painter, as well as being a great authority on the Baxter State Park up around Katahdin.

Jake "histed" himself up on the corner of the bench and busied himself at something or another. I had introduced these two men and they hit it off.

George Hand asked me if I would undertake to carve a pair of six-foot wingspread American eagles. I asked him what they were to be used for. He told me that they were to go on the pilot houses of a big ocean-going tug and a big dredge his company operated in the Gulf of Mexico.

I thought this over for a moment and said that I would undertake such a commission, but not that big. I said that a six-foot eagle mounted on the pilot house of a tug would spread enough sail so that if the tug got into one of the big blows they get in the Gulf, the next thing they knew the Eagle would take off with the tug in its talons.

George insisted that the carvings be done as large as this. I said I thought it would be a good idea if I drew up a couple of sketches of these birds, one with a four-foot wingspread, the other with a six-foot wingspread, and let the head of the house choose which one he wanted. Which was finally agreed upon. I told George that I would send along an estimate of the cost of both of these birds, too.

So, that seemed to satisfy both of us, and George took off. Jake and I talked some about the project at hand and he went back to Damariscotta. The next day I got an impressive-looking package in the mail from Jake. Its contents are pictured in Photo 41.

I made the four-foot eagles. It took a full three months from start to finish, and they were really big.

Some comment about various clamps may not be out of place. I have already described the long clamps used for edge glueing and you are probably familiar with the common iron or steel C clamps that are available. One of the most useful, and unfortunately scarce, kind are the old-fashioned wooden clamps made with two wooden screws and two wooden jaws such as are shown in Photo 42. I don't think these are made any longer. I got the ones I use at a country auction

Photo: Flye

Photo 42   The old-fashioned wood jaw and screw clamp in use.

years ago. I think I paid half a dollar for the lot. There were six
of them offered up for kindling.

They are heavy and clumsy for small work, but what a job they
do if they can once be set up. My suggestion would be to scour the

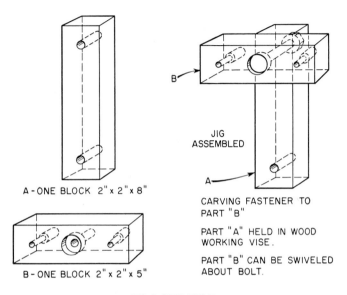

A - ONE BLOCK 2" x 2" x 8"

B - ONE BLOCK 2" x 2" x 5"

JIG
ASSEMBLED

CARVING FASTENER TO
PART "B"

PART "A" HELD IN WOOD
WORKING VISE.

PART "B" CAN BE SWIVELED
ABOUT BOLT.

PROCEDURE

Drill two ⅜-inch holes in part A, 1 inch in from either end on centerline.

Drill one ⅜-inch hole across centerlines on B. Counterbore to ½-inch with
1-inch bit.

Drill two 3/16-inch holes on centerline on B—about 3 inches apart on centers.

Counterbore these holes on face *opposite* the 1-inch counterbored center hole,
using ⅜-inch counterbore to depth of 1 inch.

Use 2-inch #10 round-head wood screws to hold carving.

Assemble both parts of jig with ⅜-inch x 5-inch carriage bolt, nut, and washer.

Figure 7-2 THE VISE JIG

countryside for them. The old cabinet shops used them, blacksmiths
used them, old boat builders used them. Mine are not for sale.

One thing you should bear in mind—the work must be held firmly
in place on the bench top. I have improvised a means of holding the

heads of eagles and such in the vise by a gadget that works out very well. I have tried to show it in Figure 7-2. Variations of the same theme can be worked out in your own shop, lacking other hold-down means.

I have found that, to facilitate the process of bosting out, mounting the "broad" gouges on long handles makes the work a lot easier (Photo 44). You can make your own handles and use short sections of brass or copper pipe for the ferrules. The ferrules prevent the tang of the tool from splitting the handle. I suggest you do not try to drive these long-handled tools; they are too difficult to guide. More care in their use will have to be exercised, for the reason that they enable you to make heavier cuts than shorter-handled tools do.

All carving tools can be made to make different kinds of cuts, each kind depending upon the angle that the cutting edge of the tool is held with reference to the stock. By rotating the handle of the tool as the cut is made—not laterally, but along the axis of the handle—the cut can be made to look as though it were twisted. I call this sort of a cut a "wind." I may be wrong in this term. It is difficult to describe in words. By rotating the end of the handle about laterally, a still entirely different kind of a cut is made. These are tricks that you learn as you go along.

Photo: Flye

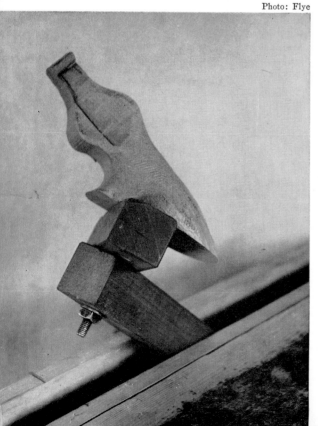

Photo 43 The vise jig in use, supporting partially bosted out eagle head. (Note the riffler marks on this portion of the carving.)

Photo: Flye

Photo 44 Bosting out with broad gouge. Note the use of the hold-down shown in drawing, Figure 7-1.

There is a tool on the market that looks to me as if it would be an extremely useful and valuable adjunct to the carver's bench; it is called a "power arm." Sculpture Associates has it for sale. Let me say here the reason I refer to this company is that it happens that theirs is the only thoroughly illustrated catalogue of carving tools I have seen. I have bought tools from them and like them.

I have not used the "power arm" in my work for the reason that I have fallen into a rut, I guess, and use the techniques that worked out well in previous experiments or on carvings. I could say here, I suppose, that I am come upon parlous times.

In bosting out the outside of comparatively large pieces where no

Photo: Flye

Photo 45 Finishing off the profile with a spoke shave. Set the blade for a fine
cut in this process.

internal cuts are to be made and where no fine detail work is to be
done, it frequently happens that a great deal of excess stock can be
more readily removed with the draw shave than with the chisel. This
tool, used properly, is a versatile one and, with some practice, can be
used for many purposes in the carver's shop. It may not be orthodox
to use it in this way, but if the results justify the means, then do so.
I should, perhaps, call attention to one drawback of this tool; it has
to be pulled toward you. It should be razor sharp and, if care is
taken to draw it through the wood with constant pressure—the blade
held at a slight skew to the run of the cut—there should be no danger
that the tool edge will leave the wood and suddenly damage either you
or the carving.

The spoke shave is also a useful device (Photo 45). This tool can
be used to great advantage in making cuts if they are long, sweeping
curves or straightaway cuts on the edge of the carving. As a matter
of fact, if the pattern of the periphery of the finished piece should be

round or oval, it is the only tool I know that you can use to reduce the edge of the piece to the design line advantageously. It, too, is a tricky tool. The blade should be set so as to take off thin shavings. Do not try to take heavy cuts with the spoke shave—it refuses to work that way. It is primarily a finishing tool, as its name implies.

These two tools should be in everyone's shop, in my opinion. If you have them, try out several different pieces of stock under them to see for yourself which tool will work best for the particular cut you want to make. As in all instances, to use edged tools effectively, they must be kept very sharp, clean from gums, and properly set in the tool holder or in your hand.

I have stressed this business of using great care with these various tools. I have done so on purpose. All edged tools are potentially dangerous even in the hands of a highly skilled artisan. I know from my own experience in working with them that nicks and cuts on your fingers, on the back of your hands, and even on your wrists are too easily come by not to call attention to this fact. I do not mean to scarehead the fact. You can learn one of two ways: by precept or by sad experience.

Photo 46 Pierced work. Repair of an ancient Chinese scholar's scroll. The light portion shows the repair insert. An interesting and typical difference change in the symmetry of the design. (*Courtesy Mortimer Graves, West Newbury, Massachusetts*)

Photo 47 Pierced work. First step boring the holes inside the sections to be removed.

Photo 48 Pierced work. The webs between the borings are cut away. Second step.

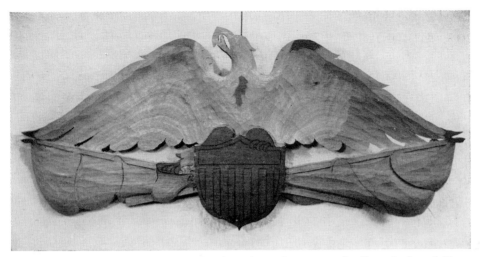

Photo 49 Pierced work. The piercings have been pared off to designed lines. Here further bosting out has been done on the carving. Note the irregularity of the profile of the Eagle's mouth.

Photo 50 Pierced work. The completed carving with all details carved and modeled. Ready for gilding and polychroming. (*Courtesy Mrs. E. R. Freeman, Damariscotta, Maine*)

Have respect for the tools of your endeavor, but don't fear them.

In the final analysis, the greater care that is taken in bosting out, in profiling, and in stopcutting a carving, the better the final results will be when you start the detail carving.

Some tips on this bosting business. Don't hurry. Check the plan against the finished planes. Check the depth of your cuts. Keep the final design of the piece in the back of your mind so that you don't overcarve. Stop work on the piece if you think you have gone far enough. Before you remove the carving from the hold-down, be sure that you have made all the rough cuts necessary to develop the internal planes of the piece. If you think that you can improve on the appearance of the piece by more bosting, wait and see. If you can, then do so. If you can't, let well enough alone. After all, it is in the art of bosting out where the final form is developed. The detail carving is the frosting on the cake.

It is possible that you may wish to undertake the complicated process of making pierced carvings (Photo 46). This is the phase of the work where all the stock is cut entirely away from the front of the carving (the face) through to the back of the carving. In other words, irregular holes.

The photographs (Photos 47–50) of the Salem Eagle and Banners illustrate this phase of the work.

Piercing can be done two ways. If you are working on stock less than an inch in thickness and are skilled in the use of the mallet and chisel, the holes can be developed in much the same manner as "sinkings"—that is, holding the tool vertically, mallet the tool into the wood, removing the surplus stock within the outline until the hole goes through the stock.

The other and easier way to do it—in thicker stock certainly—is to drill or bore (with the bit brace and bit) a series of holes around the edge of the desired hole within the outlines, leaving a space of ⅛ to ³⁄₁₆ inch between the holes. These webs will prevent the stock in the center from fracturing away from the rest of the piece and thus crowding the tools you are working with. After all the holes are drilled or bored, the webs that hold the surplus stock in place can be sheared off with the quarter-inch skew chisel. Some care must be taken to see that, in boring, the holes are vertical. Care with the skew chisel is necessary to keep the cut vertical. Make the rough cuts for pierced

Photo: Flye

Photo 51 Finishing off the sides of a piercing with the skew chisel.

work before you bost out the outline. You can carve across the holes readily enough.

To finish off the sides of a piercing, use the properly shaped tool to fit the outline and cut across the grain with the tool held at a slight skew to the face of the carving—all the while being sure the tool is held vertically (Photo 51). To make the final smoothing up of the piercing, use sandpaper. It all sounds complicated, but if you try a piercing in some waste stock by following the steps outlined above you will see it really isn't as difficult as words lead you to believe.

Rifflers are files especially designed for use on wood or stone or metal. They are made in a variety of shapes and sizes. When using them, don't forget that the action of a file is to scour off the surface. The depth of cut will depend upon the pressure on the tool. In addition to shaped rifflers, the woodworker's rasp is a most useful adjunct to the carver. Oftentimes in bosting out projecting parts of a compound carving I use the rasp to remove the final stock. It is faster than using gouges or chisels on irregular curves.

You cannot make finished cuts with rifflers or rasps. The filed surfaces will have to be carved with the properly shaped tools.

After the bosting has been completed, the next step is to finish off the profile of the carving. To do this, remove the bosted piece from the hold-down and put it in the woodworker's vise. This is why you do not attempt to do any finished carving on the piece.

To finish up the profile, use variously shaped chisels that best fit the curves of the outline and carefully pare off the stock so that all saw marks are removed and the profile has been reduced to the outline that you have designed. The care with which the outline is developed will determine the appearance of the finished piece. In some cases, it may be impossible to use a chisel to finish off certain parts. In this case, use rifflers that come closest to fitting the section. File off the surplus stock and finish up with coarse and fine sandpapers.

This operation is shown in Photos 43 and 51.

Photo: Flye

Photo 52 Detail of carved chest carved in bas-relief owned by the Author.

8

Detail Carving

One of the important steps in carving is to line out the piece after it has been bosted out and, if required, back-cut. The care with which this step is done will determine the appearance of the finished piece.

This lining out process is really a matter of laying down the guide lines for the finishing tools. The process is not necessary if the carving is designed so that it is a treatment of mass. That is, if the carver is more interested in projecting his concept of the form as an harmonious relationship of curved surfaces to the flat planes of the background of the final piece—or, in the case of a three-dimensional form, to the area or space in which the carving is to be placed. Two of the illustrations show this idea much better than words can describe it. One is the detail of a panel of a carved chest (Photo 52) and one is the formalized dolphin carved as a wall decoration (Photo 53). In these you will note a paucity of detail (see also Photo 54).

If, on the other hand, the design calls for detail carving to emphasize the finished piece, it is necessary to pencil in all the guide lines along which the finishing tools are to be run. This is shown in one of the photographs (Photo 25) of an eagle carving in process. In this project, the guide lines show where the parting tools are to be run so that the outline of the feathers can be developed. Here, the mass is less important than the detail. Were this not so, the wood from which the carving is made would have been a highly figured piece of mahogany, for the purpose of having contrasting light and dark areas of the wood relieve the plane surfaces as well as to give the finished piece a certain texture.

In order to make the point clear, I suggest you compare the two photographs (Photos 25–26) of the carving illustrated: one, the photograph of the bosted carving; and the other, the one where the bosting has been completed and where the guide lines are drawn in.

73

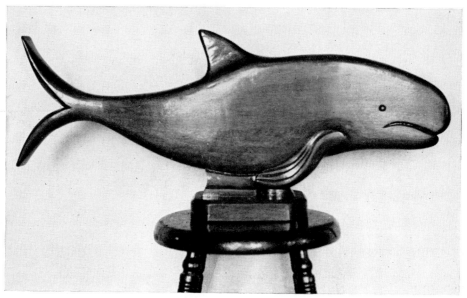

Photo 53   A carving in the round where the treatment of the mass is more important than the detail of the carving. (*Courtesy Mr. Joel H. Squier, West Tisbury, Massachusetts*)

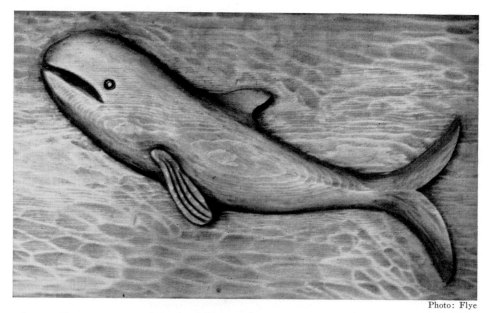

Photo: Flye

Photo 54   Another case where the detail has been sublimated to the mass. The carving is in alto-relievo. Property of the author.

Before undertaking the next step, assuming that you are going to detail the surfaces of the carving, there are three things to consider: the tools with which the detail will be developed; how the grain of the wood runs; and how the cuts with these tools will be made.

Keep in mind that any cut made on the bosted carving will have to be included in the final work. Therefore, reasonable care will have to be exercised to see that you do not overrun any of the guide lines, that the cuts are lightly made at first, and that where two cuts come together the one does not overrun the other. Try several cuts on waste stock so that any errors in tool control can be corrected without damage to the finished piece. It is a sad moment when you have to discard a carving that has progressed to the point of detail because you have spoiled it by too deep cutting, by overrunning guide lines, or by having the tool slip from the control of your hands and run at random across the piece.

I have shown an illustration of a partly finished carved piece and of the tools that I use to develop the forms of the feathers (Photo 55).

Prior to detail carving, refer to the various drawings or detailed parts of the drawings to be sure you have in mind just what it is you want to do. The projection that you have made of a typical cross section will call it to mind, that is, assuming that you made one. I

Photo 55 The tools and the partly completed detail of the feathering on an eagle. The abrupt change in the planes of the feathers when seen on the finished carving determine their outlines.

might say here, after you have worked on three or four carvings, you will find that in the preparation of your working drawings you will not find it necessary to make these projections, for the reason that your visual picture of the carving you have in mind is seen in all its dimensions. The best definition of this would be to say that you have cultivated a third-dimensional imagination. That is, you see the probable third dimension in any mental image you have of what it is you would like to do.

Coming back to the technique of detail, if the part that you are working on calls for fine, sharp work in not too heavy a relief, the outline and the internal planes can best be laid out with a quarter-inch skew chisel. Keep this tool razor sharp for this purpose. Any curved plane can be developed with this tool by either rotating the tool itself about its major axis or by rotating the tool handle about a horizontal axis or a combination of these two motions. This sounds a lot more complicated in words than it is in practice.

Here again, try trial runs on the practice block. As a matter of fact, I think that, were I to undertake to carve with a new tool, I would familiarize myself with all the possible cuts that I could presumably make with it by making a lot of cuts on the trial blocks.

The skew chisel is, perhaps, the most versatile tool in the wood carver's chest. To illustrate this point, a section of rope molding is shown where all the steps that I take to develop this form are shown (Photo 56); the whole, with the exception of the preliminary cuts made with the backsaw, being done with the skew chisel. In this case, I use a half-inch chisel.

An example of contrasting planes, flat and surfaced, are shown in the panel detail of the carved chest (Photo 52). Here all the outline was developed with the skew chisel, the long, bent, half-inch No. 17 gouge being used for the background.

In developing the detail of the wing feathers, shown in Photo 58, the parting tool is used to outline each feather; then a straight gouge, one-inch, No. 4 is used to model the surface of each feather so as to make it appear that the adjacent feather overlays the preceding one, as would be the case in actuality. The form is, of course, greatly exaggerated for the purpose of developing the final carving. It is artistic license, if you like. In my work I make no attempt to have my carvings made so as to be an accurate representation of the object

Photo 56 Detail showing all steps to follow to develop rope molding. They are, left to right, as follows:

1. Lay out guide lines on center of upright edge of stock with dividers and bevel square—¾-inch centers—or same width as stock. 2. Using tenon saw, make cuts across edge, the whole length of piece. 3. Make cuts down face of stock the whole length of stock—each of the successive steps the same. 4. With skew chisel, make diagonal cut to bottom of saw scarf, on edge. 5. Make skew cut opposite #4. 6. Make skew cut on face. 7. Make opposite cut on face. 8. Make skew cut on corners. 9. Make modeling cuts on edge. 10. Make modeling cuts on face. 11. Make very light rolling cuts to finish modeling as desired. It takes about an hour to complete 1 foot.

Photo 57 Two pieces of rope molding. The top section shows the associated molding for a cornice (see page 37, Photo 21). The lower section shows a variation of the same theme.

Photo: Flye

Photo 58 An American Eagle. The modeling of the feathers of this carving
best illustrates the use of the broad gouge—1 inch, #4—and the parting tool
in finish detail carving. This carving measures, across, wing to wing—31
inches; height, 24 inches; length, 36 inches. (*Courtesy, U. S. Senator Frederick G. Payne, Waldoboro, Maine*)

I have chosen as my theme. My eagles, for instance, are not ornitholog-
ically correct. The carving is only a similitude of the living bird.

Should you wish to make a replica of a natural object—for instance,
an eagle—it would be necessary to have such a bird as a model. Personally, I can't see keeping a tamed eagle at hand for this purpose;
besides, it's against the law here in Maine.

To outline the various planes in the finished piece, the skew chisel
or the parting tool can be used. This process is done by following
the drawn-in or guide lines on the plane surfaces of the bosted-out
carving. I prefer to use the parting tools for this purpose in most
cases. The reason for this is that the tool makes a "V" cut, that is, it
defines both sides of the cut. In using the skew chisel for this purpose
it is necessary to hold the tool so that the cutting edge is at an angle
of perhaps seventy degrees to the plane of the stock. The same cut
must be made on the opposite side of the cut with the tool held at the

Photo 59 A splendid American Eagle carved by Samuel McIntire of Salem, Massachusetts, in 1804, now owned by the Lynn Historical Society with whose permission this and the picture of the bill of sale are used.

It is interesting to note how little the art and technique of detail carving has changed in one hundred and fifty-three years by comparing this photograph with that of the American Eagle, shown in Photo 58, carved last year for Senator Payne.

Photo: Richard Merrill

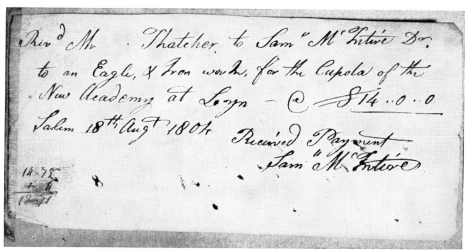

Photo: Richard Merrill

Photo 60 Bill of Sale for (American) Eagle carved by Samuel McIntire of Salem, Massachusetts. (*Courtesy Lynn Historical Society*)

79

Photo: Flye

Photo 61   Using the skew chisel for detailing the mouth and beak on an eagle's
   head.   The vise jig can be seen under my left hand and in the woodworker's
   vise.

same angle but in the opposite direction.   This process is shown in
Photo 61.

Great care must be used with either of these tools to see that a
long, running cut is made rather than a series of short, jerky cuts.
The latter result in irregular profiles.   Each stop made with the tools
makes a distinct mark on the face of the cut.

All of this sounds complicated in words, but again, if you will try
these tools on a practice block, the results will be seen.   The skew
chisel requires a greater skill in its use for this purpose than the parting tool.   The reason: the stock is apt to fracture alongside the tool
mark.

Assuming that all of the profiling cuts have been made along the
guide lines, that all the back cuts have been made to develop the

profiles of the raised areas of the carving, the next step is to model the outlined surfaces. This is done with one of the gouges. It may well be that the modeled planes are to be left smooth with few, if any, tool marks left on their surfaces. It may be that you want to leave some tool marks to relieve the plainness of the finished surfaces for texture. If the first result is desired, the broader the gouge, the smoother the effect.

If a textured surface is desired, a narrower gouge should be used. The degree of texture is developed by the shape of the gouge. Here again, the exact shape of the tool to be used is best developed by using the gouge on a practice block to see if the resulting cut is the sort you want to make for the textured effect. Various degrees of definition can be done with the same tool by winding, that is, rotating, the tool about its axis as the cuts are made or by holding it so as to make a skew cut, or a combination of both of these. Just how this texture is to look after all the cuts are made is left pretty much up to the carver.

Photo: Dr. R. B. Henning

Photo 62 A Bremen Eagle and Banner carved by the author that illustrates the change in planes of the wing feathering. (*Courtesy Dr. R. B. Henning*)

There are no hard-and-fast rules. Trial cuts will determine the degree of wind or skew you may want to use.

I suggest that two facts be kept in mind: one, that all cuts made in this process may well be final cuts; the other, that it is your carving and you can do what you want to. The choice is yours.

If, after the various planes of the carving are modeled, you want greater contrasts between the planes, it may be done by using the parting tool to increase the depths of the outline cuts. Here again, there are no hard-and-fast rules. Your taste will determine to what degree you want to develop the contrasts.

In the case of a bas-relief, no great contrast should be made between the planes and the outlines, in depth. The sharpness of the outline cuts will determine the degree of contrast. The more vertically the parting tool or the skew chisel is held to the face of the stock, the sharper the outline, hence the greater the contrast.

There will be instances in making certain carvings where it is advantageous to have some contrast made in the outline cut—where, in other words, you want to shade one plane of the carving into another. The technique here is to decrease the depth and angle of the outline cut by rotating the parting tool and by lifting it from the stock as the tool is run on the scribed line. Again, practice cuts will show you the degree of wind and lift to give you the effect that you want.

Keep in mind that, here again, it is better to take a lot of light cuts than to try to make a few heavy cuts to develop the degree of shading and texture that you want to bring out; and that razor sharp tools are easier to manipulate than just plain sharp ones.

It may seem that I am harping on one string too long when I talk about sharp tools. I do it for this reason—dull tools are dangerous, do not make clean, sharp cuts, are harder to work and are not easily manipulated in anything but soft butter. I have made it a rule to strop the tools that I expect to use in the course of the day's work before I start. It may well be that I have not used the tools in the work I did the day before, but on general principles it is easier to be sure the tools are stropped up than to make a series of running cuts only to find that the edges of the cuts are fractured rather than cut cleanly.

One of the reasons that I prefer to work in mahogany is that in making long, running cuts on the face of the stock, with sharp tools the cuts can be made with the same facility across or against the grain. To digress a moment from finishing cuts—when you are designing the carving, keep it in mind that no matter what carving stock you intend to use, carving into the end grain of any stock is the most difficult part of the work. Try to design and lay out the work so that this is avoided, if at all possible. There will be instances where it cannot be avoided. In this case, make light cuts, holding the tool at a slight angle to the face of the stock, take very light cuts using steady pressure on the tool handle, and be satisfied with small progress as you work.

What you are doing, of course, in cutting into end stock, is trying to cut at an acute angle across the ends of the wood fibres. An apt simile would be to say that you are cutting into the end of a piece of rope. These cuts can be made, they can be smooth and accurate, if sufficient care and time are taken to make them. They cannot be heavy or done hurriedly.

After the finishing cuts have been made, the final form and the shading are done. The carving can be either left as it is with the texture of the surface as it comes from the tool, or you may wish to smooth off some of the sharper lines of demarcation. In the latter case, use very fine sandpaper—not less than No. 4 Ought grit. Do not try to hurry the process. Here again, light passes across the stock will give you better effects than heavier ones. The fine paper will not scour marks in the finished surfaces and the results will be more pleasing than if heavier or coarser sandpaper is used.

It is difficult at this long range to tell you exactly what tools to use, how to use them, and what the finished carving will look like. If you are not sure which tool to use for a given effect, try out different shapes, different winds and angles, until you get the results you think will be most effective. It's your carving and you are the only one who knows what it is you want to do. You are the one who has to be pleased with the results and, if it satisfies you, I would leave well enough alone, once you have decided you are going to write "Finis" to the piece.

Here I would like to make a comment. Any creative work that is undertaken to present an idea can be overworked. When this happens, the final result will invariably be stiff, awkward, and less pleasing to the beholder than would be the case where the work has been done with a feeling of freedom and pleasure in its execution.

One day this past summer I was modeling the feathers on the wings of an eagle when a stranger wandered into the shop and began asking questions. I have made it a rule to continue with my work until I find out whether the visitor is seriously interested in the sort of work I do or if he (or she) is there out of curiosity. If the former, I willingly stop work and discuss the carving at hand and the reasons for it.

If the latter, I usually keep on with what I am doing. You can lose a lot of valuable time answering questions that are of a general nature if you stop work to satisfy curiosity. So I kept on making the long sweeps and this man watched me for some little while. I could see that he was fascinated with the way the cuts developed. Finally he asked me if he could try a cut . . . "it looks so easy."

I replied, "Sure, if you want to buy the eagle, you can."

What else could I say?

It so happens that people will sometimes ask you quite impertinent questions, too. I had four women come into the shop some years ago who offered advice about my work. I didn't mind. I kept on working. I guess they were trying to show each other how much they knew about my work and why I was doing it all wrong. Some of their

Photo: Flye

Photo 63 A seagull. Wood sculpture in tiger maple by Charles G. Chase. This and the two following photographs of his work show the radical changes made by using modern techniques and tools as compared to the traditional methods. Both result in decorative interpretations of ideas in wood. (*Courtesy Charles G. Chase, Wiscasset, Maine—Sculptor*)

Photo 64 An osprey sculptured in black walnut. Here the grain of the wood is part of the design. Note that the feathers of the bird form are sublimated to the design. Another sculpture by Charles G. Chase. Used with his permission.

Photo: Douglas Photo Shop

Photo: Flye

Photo 65 A greater yellowlegs sculpted in myrtle by Charles G. Chase. Here again the wood markings are part of the design. In these three photographs showing bird sculpture the work is done from a solid block. Mr. Chase's approach to the decorative qualities of the characteristics of the woods is particularly emphasized. The results are sculptures of extraordinary beauty. (*Courtesy Charles G. Chase*)

remarks were quite amusing and some not quite so funny. I might say here that all of them looked as if somebody had thrown a lot of curves at them that got stuck in all the wrong places.

The shortest and loudest of these women finally asked me why I didn't carve the human form divine and stop work on eagles. I thought this over for a moment and decided I had taken about enough. So, I very carefully put the tool in my hand back into the tray, walked around the four women and looked them all over very carefully from head to foot. They got slightly embarrassed as I did so. I walked back to where I had been working, picked up the carving tool, started to make another cut, stopped and quietly asked one question: "Whose?"

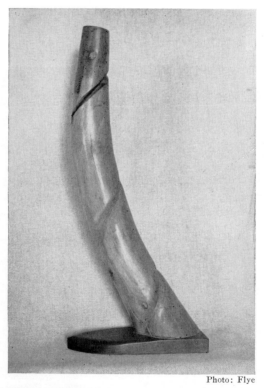

Photo: Flye

Photo 66 An abstract carving in the round: "Man's Aspirations." Owned by the Author.

9

Making a Stern Transom Carving

I have tried to cover all the steps involved in making a wood carving for decoration in the home or office or in similar places where the problems of its production were concerned with the profile of the piece and where the treatment of the face of the carving contributed to the final appearance of the finished work.

The production of a carving used to decorate the stern transom of a yacht is a much more involved and complicated process. I think that in order to make such a carving I would try to undertake a less complicated carving first, make all the mistakes on that, learn the full use of the various tools and techniques I have tried to describe and then undertake the more complicated processes outlined in the following paragraphs.

Nearly all yacht transoms are curved. If the one you want the carving for is not, the previously described techniques apply. If it is

(text continues p. 92)

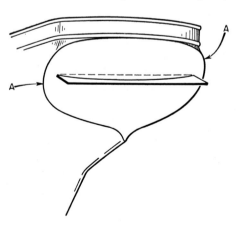

Transom curve has been scribed off and template cut to fit curve of transom.

Dotted line shows inner edge of template before cutting.

Be sure to take off outboard profile of transom on paper: A-A, etc.

Figure 9-1

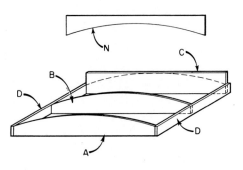

Figure 9-2

N—Template scribed from transom, Figure 9-1

A—6-inch board cut to line scribed from template; "B" ditto

C—6-inch board scribed but not cut

D—3-inch stringers to which A-B-C are nailed

This shows false transom frame. ¼-inch plywood to be nailed on top of curved sections.

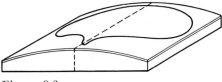

Figure 9-3

Transom is outlined on false transom. Shellac lines. Be sure to index centerline.

Figure 9-4 SUGGESTED DESIGN FOR TRANSOM CARVING

The eagle and name and hailing port banners would require not less than 5 pieces to make.

The rope molding would require probably 12 pieces to make.

This one will be used to illustrate the various processes.

It will consist of two parts for the shield, one part for each banner.

Figure 9-5 SUGGESTED DESIGN FOR STERN TRANSOM CARVING

1. Clip stock to length. Joint at A-A'. Glue and clamp.

2. When glue is set, layout design, profile out, and finish edges.

Note: Be sure grain of wood in both pieces runs the same way as shown by arrows.

Figure 9-6

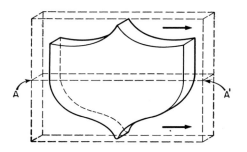

1. Block up edges so block is level. Be sure centerlines coincide.

2. Scribe both top and bottom edges.

3. Back-cut across carving blank to scribed lines. (Dotted line is outline for carving blank before profile is cut. Piece to be scribed is *profiled blank*.)

4. Follow same procedure for banners.

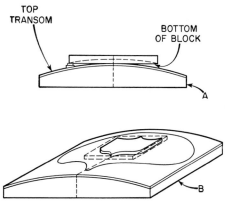

Figure 9-7 POSITION OF CARVING BLOCK ON FALSE TRANSOM FOR SCRIBING BACK CUT

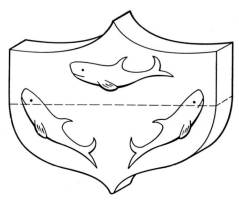

Figure 9-8 BACK CUT COMPLETED AND DESIGN LAID ON FOR
CARVING FACE OF BLOCK. (Dotted line shows glued joint.)

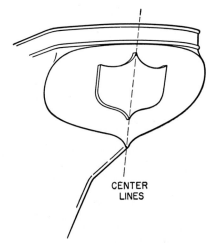

1. Scribe outline for errors.

2. Reduce errors with rifflers or rasps
for perfect fit.

3. Follow same procedure with banners.

4. Do not detail-carve until these
steps are completed.

Figure 9-9 CHECKING PROFILED BLANK ON TRUE TRANSOM FOR
FIT

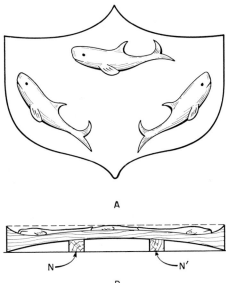

1. Stop-cut to outline.
2. Bost out as shown in B.
3. Bottom off bosted face.
4. Model dolphins in bas-relief or mezzo-relievo.

Use support blocks N-N' while bosting and carving.

Suggested finish background deep blue or vermilion. Gild dolphins.

Figure 9-10   CARVING THE DESIGN

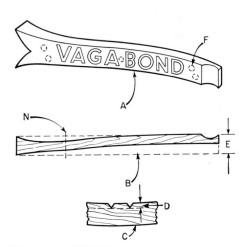

A—Finished pieces.

B—Side view: Reduce face from "N" to end to about same thickness.

C—Depth of cut for letters at D about $3\frac{1}{6}$ inches.

Suggest banners be finished in same color as shield. Gild letters.

Figure 9-11   MAKING AND LETTERING BANNERS

curved, the process is, as I have said, much more complicated. All the skill of a wood joiner, of a designer, and of a carver are called upon to produce such a piece of work.

These are the steps I follow in such work (refer to Figures 9-1 through 9-11):

Determine the radius of the curve of the transom. Make a mock-up of the transom. Make a profile of the transom. Make the design. Get out the various parts for the carving. Profile the work, back-cut to fit the mock-up, assemble the parts and fit to the true transom approximately. Then bost out. Join the parts again (using wood screws for this purpose). Try the parts again for fit on the true transom. Back-cut again to fit to close limits. Finish-carve the parts and reassemble. Fit again to the true transom, this time to exact limits. Joint, fasten and glue up the finished carving, finish the surfaces and apply the carving to the transom permanently. And there you are—you hope.

To determine the curve or radius of the transom it is not enough to draw this curve on the drawing paper, for this reason: there are always variations in the finished transom due to errors in production in the yacht yard, some distortion in the stock after the hull is done and the stresses are applied to the transom when the various braces are removed.

To take off the true profile of the stern transom I use a thin piece of pine, usually a long, pine clapboard. Hold the thin edge of the board against the center, horizontally, of the transom and with the carpenter's scribe run a line along the face of the board. The pencil marker will make this line so that it corresponds with the irregularities of the transom. Cut the stock out along this line with the draw shave, finishing off with the spoke shave so that when this template is held against the transom in the same place where it was scribed, all faces of the curve of the template touch the face of the transom.

Then try the template at the upper part of the transom, note any discrepancies with the scribe; then do the same thing with the bottom of the transom. If the discrepancies are less than an eighth of an inch, do not try to correct them. It is not necessary. If they are greater, try to hit a happy medium as this profile is for the mocked-up or temporary transom you will build for use in your shop.

The second step is to take off the outline (or profile) of the transom as it exists on the yacht.

I do this by placing large sheets of brown paper over the transom so they cover the piece with some overlapping of the edges. I fasten the paper to the hull with masking tape. It comes off the paint work without leaving any gum. If two or more pieces of paper are required to cover the transom, I usually lay the upper sheet over the lower and lay on two or three pencil lines so they cross the overlaps, one in the center and one at either side. Then I use a soft pencil and trace off the profile of the transom, using great care to see that I get it as exact as I can.

To make the mock-up, lay the piece of stock you used to get the radius of the transom on a wide pine board. Trace the curve on the face of the board. Repeat this process until three boards are scribed. Then develop the curve, being sure that the bottom edges of all the boards to be profiled out are straight. Remove the stock with the draw and spoke shaves. Check the curve against the template. Draw a line one quarter inch below the curve and finish to that line. Assemble the profiled boards in such manner that they are held firmly in a vertical position. Apply a piece of ¼-inch plywood to the curved faces of the boards and nail in place with lath nails. Before nailing, put the template on the face of the plywood to be sure that it fits snugly. This, then, becomes the surface to which you will back-cut the carving and on which the outline of the transom is drawn as well as the design for the carving.

The next step is to transfer the profile or the outline of the transom to the mocked-up section. Do this with carbon paper the same way you transfer the carving design to the block. Darken this outline with a soft pencil. Then shellac it to prevent it from smudging as you work on the mock-up to fit the various pieces of the carving to it.

Transfer the outline of the transom to your drawing paper on which you intend to make your design. At the top of your drawing paper, lay out the curve of the transom from the template. Draw in the chord.

Then make your design, keeping well within the limits of the outline of the transom. Here, I would suggest that you make the design on a piece of tracing paper so that you can, from time to time, lift the drawing away from the board and lay it on the mock-up to see if it is what you want to make. There is some difference in the appearance and dimension of the design when seen in a flat plane from when the design is placed on the curved plane of the transom.

After you have roughed out the outline of the proposed carving on the drawing paper, extend vertical lines from the extremities of the design and from the center of the design to the top of the paper so that these vertical lines cross the chord and intersect the arc (which represents the true transom). You now can see how much or how little the carving blank will have to be back-cut and how much additional stock must be added (built up) to give you the proper thicknesses with which to work.

This step can be done mathematically, I suppose, but I find that the trial-and-error method works out quite as well.

By studying the proposed design and the varying thicknesses of stock necessary to develop the carving you will have it fixed in your mind just what is required of you to do the work.

In the illustrations I have prepared for this phase of the work I have used a relatively simple form, that of a shield on which dolphins are carved in mezzo-relievo, for the reason that the principles involved in this sort of carving apply to any other form as well. My feeling is that for the first endeavor you are going to use a simple, straightforward design that is well within your capacity to produce. Do not try to undertake a large, involved piece of work that will exceed your capacity to make. Nothing is more discouraging to do than to come up against a problem in your work that is beyond your knowledge and skill to overcome.

After all, if you want to make a more detailed carving later on you can sell the yacht and start again. Or you can remove the prior piece and replace it with a more ambitious work.

After you have established the form of the carving and indicated some of the detail, determine how you are going to build up the carving blank if that is necessary. This you do from the measurements on the chord. I allow at least one half inch more stock than is required at any point on the block. More, if it works out that way. The block can be built up from the bottom or from the top. In any case, when the several pieces are to be jointed, follow the same processes as are described elsewhere in the text.

Having decided upon the design, make a complete drawing of it. Detail the drawing, trace in the outline or profile of the transom from your layout paper and place this on the mock-up. If you are satisfied with the drawing, lay out the profiles on the carving block. A word of advice—do not glue the carving block together if more than one piece of stock has to be used. Hold the various parts together with counter-bored screws, for the reason that, when you profile the block, it is easier to profile out each piece than the whole thing. You will find that it is easier to disassemble the parts than to work from a solid block for some of the following steps: bosting out, back-cutting and detail carving.

After the block has been profiled, place the assembled block on the mock-up and lay in the curves on the profile with the carpenter's scribe. Do this all around the carving. Separate the various pieces and back-cut each piece to approximately $\frac{3}{16}$ inch of the scribed line. Certainly not closer than that. Assemble the pieces, lay them on the mock-up, and see how nearly a fit you have come to the curve of the transom. By placing clipped ends of $\frac{3}{16}$ inch Prestwood under the block, set the scribe to that dimension and run the line over. Here the differences will be apparent and can be corrected for a better fit.

The purpose of this surplus stock is that it gives you an opportunity to fit the bosted-out block to the actual transom. This must be done before any detail carving is undertaken. Once you have fitted the bosted block to the mock-up, take it to the yacht and fit it to the transom there. I usually pare off the profiled surfaces of the carving prior to this fitting so that, when I scribe in the outline of the true transom, I do not have any lines to divert me from back-cutting for a better fit after I have returned to the shop.

Having scribed the block to the true transom, back-cut to an eighth of an inch of the scribed line. It is essential that there be this surplus stock left in place at this stage of the game. The block can be checked against the mock-up transom as a matter of checking, but do not back-cut to fit the mock-up hereafter.

Prior to gluing the block together, be sure that all the rough work has been done: that the bosting is complete, the back-cuts made, the periphery of the carving has been pared off and smoothed up with the necessary tools. Here, be sure that the edges are as nearly vertical to the planes of the back-cut stock as you can make them.

Photo 67 The eagle is detail-carved; the back cutting and fitting are being checked against the transom prior to painting and gilding the eagle. (*Courtesy Yachting Magazine*)

The next step is to line out the block, then separate the various pieces, glue and assemble, screw them together and, if necessary, apply clamps for a good, tight, glued joint or joints. Wipe off surplus glue with a hot, wet cloth and set aside, after setting plugs in the counter-bored holes.

The final step, as in any other carving, is to detail-carve the block. Be sure that, when doing this, the underside of the carving is properly supported; otherwise it is possible that certain portions of the carving can be fractured off or that undue distortion of the finished carving can take place. This is most important. When the finished carving has been done, the final check for fit on the true transom is to be made.

Place the carving against the transom in its proper place and see if you have a fit. If you have, that's fine; if you haven't, joint the back of the carving to the transom with wood rasps or rifflers. This process cannot be hurried. I have found out that it is possible to place the finished face of the carving on sponge rubber pads (such as are

Photo 68 The name and hailing port banners are being checked for fit on the transom prior to carving letters and finish painting and gilding. (*Courtesy Yachting Magazine*)

Photo 69 The finished transom. The rope molding was made in twelve parts, the eagle in three parts, the banners in three parts. This transom was fitted in place on the ketch "Kokua" owned by Stanley Livingston, Jr., of Providence. (*Courtesy Yachting Magazine*)

sold for gardening) while rasping off the back of the carving in this final finishing fit. This prevents fracture of the detail. No clamps are necessary, but a spare set of hands is, if you have them handy. I never have, so I hold the work in place with my foot or leg or elbow or even sit on it if I have to. The important thing is to get a good close fit.

Having done this, handle the carving with great care from here on in. The next step is, of course, to finish the carving with color or gold leaf, or whatever is chosen.

There are some points that I suggest be kept in mind. Do not try to design a carving where a lot of fine detail work is involved. The detail will be lost in the overall picture. Avoid small sections, if possible. These are likely to be broken off in the course of time. Be reasonably careful to see that a watertight joint between the back of the carving and the transom is made with some of the plastic seals that are available for marine work by applying this to the back of all parts and wiping off the surplus.

To fasten the carving to the transom use brass or "Everdure" wood screws of a suitable size. I set these screws into a counter-bored and

Photo 70   The completed carving of the ancient mariner shown in the drawings
        on the right. "A caricature of all the masters and mates I sailed with when I
        was a boy." (*Courtesy Mr. Joel H. Squier*)

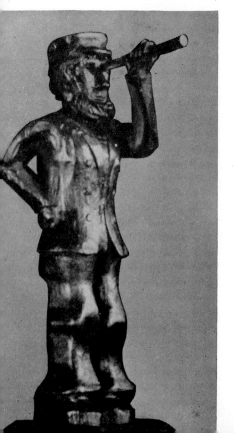

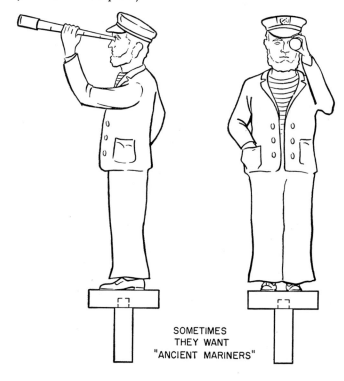

SOMETIMES
THEY WANT
"ANCIENT MARINERS"

plugged hole and then pare off the plug after it is set. To set these plugs use Duco Cement, sparingly. The ends of the plugs can be finished in the same manner as the rest of the carving in which they are placed.

The final step is to christen the carving with the vehicle of your choice. I find a bottle of ale applied in judicious amounts to the inner man does an adequate job.

And be prepared to make other carvings for your friends, too.

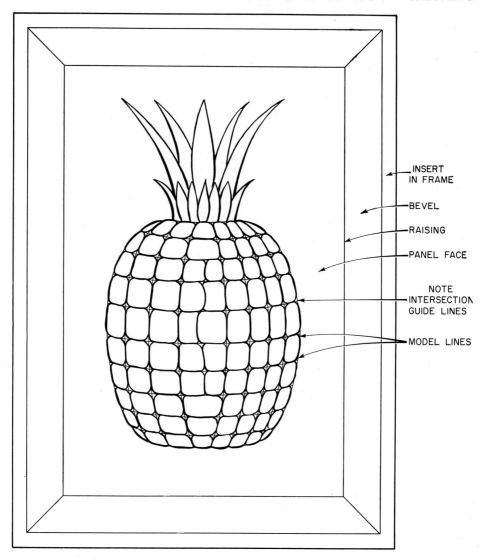

INSERT
IN FRAME

BEVEL

RAISING

PANEL FACE

NOTE
INTERSECTION
GUIDE LINES

MODEL LINES

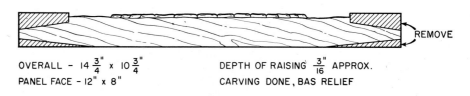

REMOVE

OVERALL – 14 3/4" x 10 3/4"   DEPTH OF RAISING 3/16" APPROX.
PANEL FACE – 12" x 8"   CARVING DONE, BAS RELIEF

Figure 10-1 LAYOUT FOR PINEAPPLE PROJECT

10

Making a Carved Panel

I have tried to stress the fact in the foregoing chapters that it is advisable for anyone starting a new venture, such as wood carving, to start with a simple design. With this in mind, I have shown the various steps that can be followed to make a relatively simple carving; one that will call for certain skills in the use of both the carpenter's tools (a more fitting name would be the casemaker's tools) and the carving tools, as well.

All the steps involved in this small problem are fully shown in the accompanying illustrations, from the layout of the design, the steps taken to make the design in plan and cross section, the method of transfer, the preparation of the carving block, the transfer of the design to the panel face, and all the succeeding steps necessary to complete the finished work.

A description of these various steps follow in the order in which they are executed.

First the drawing. The overall outline of the panel is drawn to full size. The outline of the panel raising is next drawn. The index lines are drawn. One half the design is roughly sketched in. The tracing off of this half is done next and then transferred to the opposite side.

Before I go further, I should make this comment, I think. It has been my observation that in Nature there are no duplicates. No two sides of any natural object are exactly the same; no two apples are exactly alike, no two waves are ever the same. Nature is the vast storehouse of infinite variety. This being so, any representation of a natural object should have variants, as well.

Back to our muttons. After the outline of the pineapple is traced off and the section lines are indicated, complete both halves of the drawing, varying the detail freely. These lines are indicative of what you want the finished carving to look like—only. They do not have to be followed exactly.

The next step is to prepare the panel in cross section. Note this: all the following steps are done with hand tools only.

Search out in your stockpile a piece of dry, white pine board about 11 inches wide by about 16 inches long. Be sure the stock is clear of knots, shakes, and sapstreaks. Lay out the actual overall size of the panel—that is, width 10¾ by 14¾ inches. Plane both edges down to the width dimension. Lay off its length and square the ends on the layout lines with the panel saw. Be sure that the ends are square-cut vertically, as well. (The panel saw is the fine-toothed crosscut saw.) Plane the surface of the panel with the grain to smooth the surface for the next step which is to lay out the raisings.

Using the backsaw (or tenoning saw), cut along the outline of the raising to a depth of ¼ inch, first across the grain at either end, then with the grain on either side (Photo 71). Hold the panel in place on the bench top by means of two thin strips of wood nailed with brads to the bench top—the strips to go across one end and along one

Photo 71 Cutting along the outline of the raising. Note—the design has been transferred to the panel face.

Photo: **Flye**

Photo 72   Cutting along the saw scarf for the raisings with the one-inch firmer chisel.

Photo 73   Cutting the raising down to the scribed line.   Note the manner in which the tools are held in these photographs.   Some small skill and assurance are necessary in this cut.

side.   The best way to do this is to place the squared-up panel on the bench for guiding the position of these strips.

Use either one of two tools to carve out the stock between the extremes of the panel and the outline cuts; a one-inch firmer chisel or a one-inch skew chisel (Photos 72 and 73).   I prefer the latter, though the former is just as good.   These cuts should be made so that the cuts are first finished parallel with the face of the panel.   The next step is to mark guide lines on the sides and ends of the panel to the depth to which the edging is to be finished according to your cross-section drawing.   Always work with the grain of the piece when making cuts on the sides of the panel.   Hold the chisel at a skew (an angle) to the end of the stock when cutting across the grain.

Be sure that these cuts do not run into the sides or the ends of the raising.

Using great care, finish off the edging cuts so that they slope from the raising to the edge of the stock and to the guide lines that you have drawn.   If you use a firmer chisel, place the *face* of the tool against the stock for this purpose.   This operation is difficult and tricky, but if care is taken to remove very little stock at a time, the results will please you.   Be sure that the tool is always held at a skew in this process.

The raising done, lay on the drawing of the pineapple.   Be sure you have the inner corners of the raising indexed on your drawing and place these points over the corners of the raising.   These will position the drawing on the center of the panel.   Trace off.

The next step is to make the stopcuts along the outline of the pineapple (Photo 74).   Do this with a narrow skew chisel, holding the tool almost vertically with the face of the panel.   Go along all the outline of the drawing.   Don't try to outline all the terminal leaves at this point.   Make your first cuts lightly.   Follow this by increasing the depth of the cuts.   Next, back-cut to the outline (Photo 75).   I use a #14, ⅜-inch long bent gouge for this.   Repeat the process of outlining the carving until you have reached the depth of the carved pineapple you show in your cross section, that is, $\frac{3}{32}$ inch.   Bost out the stock between the outline and the raising edge.   Try to leave a little stock here for finishing cuts.   This will be the last portion of the carving to finish up, for this reason: as you work on the detail of

Photo 74 Stopcutting along the outline of the design with the quarter-inch skew chisel.   The raisings are completed.

Photo 75 Backcutting to the stopcuts on the outline.

Photo: Flye

Photo 76   Modeling the leaves of the pineapple; the sections have been partially
modeled out.

the surface of the pineapple, the chances are that the edge or point
of your tool will touch the bosted surface and, if this is finished before the face of the pineapple is done, you will have to remove these
tool marks.   Why repeat?

The next step is to develop the leaves of the pineapple.   Do this
by lightly outlining them with the skew chisel.   Using the ½-inch
gouge, model the planes of these leaves so that they slope in various
directions as they would in the actual fruit (Photo 76).   Don't forget
you are making a bas-relief carving; therefore, all modeling will have
to be lightly done.   The effect of the rounding of the pineapple comes
in the way in which the design has been made, not in modeling.

After the leaves have been modeled, the next step is to carve and
model the sections along the design lines (Photo 77).   This is done,
again, with the skew chisel in the manner shown.   Make the cuts

across the grain first, and then the cuts with the grain. Take care to see that your tool does not travel across the bosted section. After the section outline cuts are made, model the corners of the sections down into the outline cuts to give them the rounded effect you show in the drawing. Do this bit of modeling with the ½-inch gouge, with the face of the tool held against the face of the stock to be cut, that is, with the heel of the tool outward. This is a tricky business, but with care and patience it can be done.

The final step in modeling the fruit is to model the edge of the pineapple (Photo 78). Do this with the gouge, again being careful to make light cuts and being sure that you do not cut too far into the face of the detailed fruit. This tends to soften the outline and make it seem to flow out of the panel rather than rise abruptly.

The last step in carving is to smooth off the bosted section. Here I suggest that you use a broad gouge for this purpose. Again light cuts will be more effective than heavier ones. Overlap the tool marks

Photo: Flye

Photo 77 Finishing the modeling of the sections with the quarter-inch skew chisel.

Photo 78 Modeling the edge of the pineapple with the #14, ⅜-inch gouge.

and use great care to avoid the edge of the pineapple. Any tool mark on that portion of the carving will be apt to spoil the outline because it will be necessary to carve the mark out if you want a finished piece.

Having completed the carving, I would not sand any portion of the carved face. The edging can be sanded smooth, if you want.

Now that the panel is done, don't ask me what to do with it. Hanging it up in the shop may be the answer. It is purely a practice piece or, if you are really ambitious, you can make a duplicate and mount them as end boards in a chest or in frames to be hung in some dark corner.

My purpose in proposing this carving is that in its execution most of the tricks of the trade are used in the work.

The pineapple motif is used very freely. Its significance in architecture is that it represents an hospitable welcome to guests. One of the illustrations shows a corner cupboard I made as a gift to my wife after I had sold a Welsh dresser out from under her heirloom collection of Chelsea china in an unguarded moment of enthusiasm. As you will see, the pineapple has been used freely, as well as rope molding and the lotus flower with the Ying and the Yang of the Chinese.

Raised panels, such as the one under discussion, can be used in an infinite number of ways—for instance, as an over the mantel panel or as panels for a study. For such uses, it would be well to vary the bas-relief design on each panel to break up the similarity.

In all cases in making bas-relief carvings, the shape of the object and the appearance of roundness and depth are developed in the way the piece is designed and in the faithful execution of the carving according to the drawing. This perspective business is a funny thing. If I were a better draftsman and knew more about it, I could tell you how to do it according to the book. I do it by trial and error. If it does not look the way I want it to the first time, I do it over until it does.

In mezzo-relievo the development of perspective is a rather easier matter; in alto-relievo, quite simple. However, neither of these forms of carving is customarily used for raised panel work, except in rare instances, such as a panel that is to be placed at a point well above the eye of the beholder or where massive detail is used in all of the associated areas. The form of relief will depend upon these factors as well as upon the skill of the wood carver.

I have included, in the illustrations of wood carvings that I have made in the past, pictures of a room in which several forms of carving and cabinet work are shown. These were taken in the living room of a house in South Bristol, Maine, owned by the late Glenn Stewart, who was one of the finest men I have ever had the pleasure of knowing. It was through his interest and that of Mrs. Stewart that I really got into the serious business of wood carving.

The work shown in part took all of one winter to execute. All the work was done to my designs and I had pretty much of a free hand as to what I wanted to do.

The bookcase (Photo 79) is of some interest in that it has as decorative forms scallop shells carved in mezzo-relievo as well as intaglio. The flutings are done with a special tool called a "fluter," which is not too commonly found in a carver's chest. I hesitated to carve an elaboration on the scallop theme on the door panels and now I am

Photo: Flye

Photo 79 Bookcase showing the use of scallop shells as primary motif. Use of rope molding. All work on this bookcase is done with hand tools. (*Courtesy Mrs. Glenn Stewart*)

glad that I did not do so. The valance boards are examples of plain panels made in the manner that is set forth in this chapter. As a contrast to the bookcase, the fire frame and the mantel shelf are quite simple in design (Photo 80).

These pictures show how wood carvings can be used as decorative architectural forms in a modern setting and how they can be used in conjunction with other decorative media to enhance the beauty of a room.

Photo 80   Mantel and fire frame detail—all hand carved.   (*Courtesy Mrs. Glenn Stewart*)

Photo: Flye

11

Polychroming, Gilding, and Staining

In making bread, mixing the dough is only one step in the process. Making a carving is not necessarily the end of the job.

In these hurrying times we hate to wait for Nature to darken our work with the patina of age. So we resort to stains or color or paint or some other vehicle to give the finishing touch to the completed work.

This is an involved process and calls for some skill in the use of the best materials to accomplish whatever finish we have in mind. In my experience, carvings are wanted in gold leaf, in the natural color of the wood, some want them stained, some, as in the case of eagles, want them painted in the natural colors of the living bird. Banners are painted in many different colors; incised or raised letters are either gilded or painted. Other carvings, as in the instance of State Seals, are usually painted according to the original.

The technical terms for all these processes are as follows:

Stains. As the name implies, this is a coloring process used to darken the carving with either commercial stains or with those that are mixed in your own shop.

Painting. Generically termed polychroming. I will use this term hereafter.

Gilding. The term used to define the application of gold leaf and NOT a gilt paint. Personally I never use gilt paint. I call it a poor substitute for the original gold leaf, and in my opinion it is a lot of muck. The reason I dislike it is that it discolors and won't last either indoors or out. I have put my neck out on that one.

These are the three conventional ways to add to the attractiveness of the finished work and can be used singly or in any combination that may be desired.

STAINING

When finishing a carving in stain, I prefer to mix my own color stock, using either dry earth colors or tube colors. If the former, a deeper stain can be developed, if you remember to keep the pigments used to obtain the color stirred up thoroughly in the vehicle. The following dry colors are suggested: American vermilion, Van Dyke brown, raw sienna, raw umber, burnt sienna, burnt umber, and Indian red. All these are available in most good paint stores. They are inexpensive and will keep indefinitely if stored in pint glass Mason jars with rubber rings and glass tops.

All these colors are available in artist's tube colors ground in either oil or japan. The advantage of tube color as a stain stock is that, when the color is let down in the vehicle, it stays in suspension. Tube color costs a lot more than the dry color.

The first step in making your own stain is to mix the vehicle. My best advice is to use raw linseed oil, japan dryer, and turpentine. The amounts to use will depend upon how much of a hurry you are in. Short-set vehicle (quick drying) is obtained by increasing the amount of japan dryer used. Thinning the oil with turpentine hastens the drying process somewhat, cuts the gloss, and gives deeper penetration to the oil when applied to the wood. Since I mix my vehicle by guess and by God, I can't give any set rule to follow. I suggest you try various proportions on waste stock to see which gives you the best result. There is some slight difference in the setting process when dry versus tube color stock is used. I pay this no attention.

The vehicle being mixed (rather more than you think you will need for the job at hand), pour off some of the vehicle into a separate container for testing color.

Bear this in mind; if dry color stock is used, it must be mixed with a small quantity of vehicle before it is added to the pot. The dark colors are very strong—use small quantities. I usually start my stain by mixing some raw sienna first. This is the base color. It is a soft, light tan. The quantity used in the vehicle will determine the depth of the color—not the tone. Add judicious amounts of burnt sienna if the general tone is to be on the reddish brown side. If it is to be on the brown side with no red tones, use small quantities of Van Dyke brown for this. If it is to be a blend of the browns and reds, use some burnt sienna, Van Dyke brown, and American vermilion. For instance, in staining an ordinary-sized table the proportions I use are: 1½ cups of vehicle, about 2 tablespoons of raw sienna, then one third as much of Van Dyke brown, and a very slight amount of American vermilion. This gives a moderately deep brownish stain. Indian red will give a richer tone, if that is wanted. Burnt and raw umber are used to give a patina of age. They are essentially muddy colors in tone and should be used with great care.

It can be a very rewarding process, this mixing your own stain. Commercial stains are available. My objection to their use is that you don't know what has been used by the manufacturers to carry the color, nor do you know whether or not the colors are dyes or earthen colors. If you try to blend two or more commercial stains, you may run into a chemical incompatibility that will affect the whole appearance of the piece.

The best way to find out how to bring order out of chaos is to try several batches of stock until you have come upon the combination that is most pleasing to you. For goodness' sake, don't have the carving to which the stain is going to be applied within hailing distance of your color experiments. If dry color lands on the wood, it can't all be removed and will show up. If you use tube colors, the result is even worse.

POLYCHROMING

Polychroming is the application of tube color in one or more coats to the carving (Photo 81). Here the technique is similar to that used by any person handling colors for painting. With this exception, you are going to apply the color over prime-coated stock. Prime coating consists of applications of flat white paint. Two coats should be sufficient. Its purpose is to seal the wood against the absorption of oil and to enable you to reduce the number of coats of paint you have to use to develop the richness of the tones you think should be obtained.

Flat undercoating paints are made by most paint makers and some may be better than others. If possible, get one in which the pigment used is white lead; the vehicle, linseed oil and turpentine. The big paint companies are using more and more synthetic materials and, in some instances, these are incompatible with the natural materials. It is unfortunate, perhaps, that we do live in a synthetic age where stuff is used that beggars a layman's understanding.

If the manufacturer of the paint that you want to use does not put an intelligible (to you) formula on the outside of his paint can, don't buy it, is my advice. I feel very strongly about this mumbo jumbo that appears on the outside of the package. I haven't time to learn the art of synthetics, so that if they don't tell me that all the stuff they use is man made, I get something else.

Mixing colors to obtain the exact shade, color, and tone is an art in itself and one well worth learning. Don't be afraid to experiment. Up until now nothing you have done has been orthodox, so why not continue?

Make notes as you go along, if you are new at the business. Number your color samples and make your notes on what you did to correspond to them. This is an invaluable help if you ever want to repeat a color, a tone, a stain, or whatever it is that is to be duplicated. After some experimentation, you will find that you do things pretty much the way you did before.

Photo 81 Bremen Eagle carved in alto-relievo and polychromed in bird's natural colors. Owned by the Author.

Photo: Flye

Here again, there are no hard-and-fast rules as to what colors to use, how to use them, or whether or not this color and that should go together. It's your work; please yourself.

GILDING

The art of gilding has never, to my knowledge, been fully explained. The language used by the professional gilder is worlds apart from that used by the layman. Also it is one of the hardest jobs an inexperienced hand can undertake. It is an awful lot of fun, though, especially when you do finally get a carving gilded and look at it in awe and wonderment at your handiwork.

I will try to describe, as best I can, the steps I take to gild a carving.

The carving being completed, I apply two coats of white lead and oil paint. I mix this myself out of ground white lead, raw linseed oil, some turpentine, and some japan dryer. The consistency is about that of medium cream. It should be very thoroughly stirred. The stirring blends the lead pigments with the vehicles. I think the more it is stirred, the better it flows. Allow at least two days between coats for drying—longer if the weather is humid. Usually, not always, the proportion of oil, turpentine, and dryer are given on the can of white lead. (I buy it in 5-pound lots.) If not, then write the manufacturer for these. He will be glad to send you any information he has on this matter.

After the second coat has set and is hard to the touch (usually three to four days), I apply a slow-set oil gilding size. This can be made at home, but I have found that Hastings and Company's size is extremely good and very consistent. I apply the gilding size in such manner that there are no skips ("holidays" to the initiate) and usually do the sizing about four o'clock in the afternoon.

It takes about eighteen hours for the gilder's size to set up to a suitable tack. Tack, in this case, means the degree of stickiness. It is hard to define or explain. The nearest I can come is to say that it is the degree of stickiness that, when you touch it with your knuckle, there is a distinct feeling of the size pulling at the flesh yet not coming off the stock onto your finger. When it has reached this degree of tack you are ready to apply the gold leaf.

Gold leaf comes in books. There are twenty-five books in a pack.

The pack costs about $32.00. The leaf is supplied in either the "Board" or "Mounted" leaf. In the mounted leaf, the gold is adhered lightly to a thin tissue separator. It is used primarily for gilding on glass. Unmounted or "Board" leaf is, as its name implies, not mounted on tissue. The separators are rouged to prevent the leaf from adhering to them. The trick is to get the leaf off the rouged paper and onto the carving without having it fold out of shape. Mind you, this leaf is only two ten-thousandths of an inch thick.

Gilding *must* be done in a room where there are no drafts and where the probability of a door being suddenly opened is reduced to the irreducible minimum or else the draft will take charge and "there goes sixpence." To lift gold leaf from the book, use a fine camel's-hair, a red badger or a squirrel hair brush. I use a red badger brush one inch wide. It costs about $15.00 and is worth its weight in gold.

I have tried gilder's tips without much luck, perhaps because I am in the habit of using the brush described.

Pass the brush across your hair, if you aren't bald. If you are, I don't know what you do, but in this case try a bit of velvet. What you are trying to do is to charge the bristles with static electricity. Then expose the sheet of gold by folding back the cover and pages of the book in such a way that the whole piece of the leaf is exposed on the rouged separator. Very carefully (and be sure that your hand is steady) place the brush against the edge of the leaf, lift with a slight circular twist and, again with care, float the suspended leaf onto the face of the sized carving. It cannot be moved once it touches the tack.

Here is a suggestion. Try all these steps on a practice piece. Plan to waste four or five books of gold leaf in the process of learning the trick. After all, you are spending a rather small sum to learn a new and, to me at least, fascinating part of the business. When I started to gild, I didn't know any more about it than a Hottentot. I spent three days, and I forget how much leaf, trying to learn some of the tricks of the trade. A very gifted sign painter was in the shop not long ago and saw one of my carvings that I had just gilded. He looked at it and, turning around, offered me a job doing all his gilding. Now, that could have been a line or he really meant it. I didn't press the point—nor am I gilding his lilies.

The final step in gilding is to brush all the fractured leaf back onto the face of the carving, using the one-inch brush. Keep it moving about the surface to be sure that no voids are left; that is, no places where you didn't get the leaf on exactly as you wanted it. These skips or voids can be touched up later by reapplying the size to the spots and regilding.

Several days, perhaps four, after the gilding has been done (the time lapse is to be sure that the gilding size has made its final set and that it has hardened under the gold leaf), burnish the face of the gold with a piece of silk velvet. A piece about 8 inches square is large enough. This can be done with surgical absorbent cotton. Surgical cotton is sure to be free of any foreign matter that might scratch the gold. Do this burnishing very carefully. Don't rub, pass the velvet or cotton pad gently across the surface in the same direction. This process brings the gold up to a lustrous finish.

I feel reasonably sure that if you were to write Hastings and Company * for instructions they would be only too glad to send them to you. I didn't think of that when I "lessoned myself." There I think I was really stupid. And on some other scores as well.

If any carving which you have made is to be used out of doors, the back of the carving has to be protected from the weather as well as the face of the carving. Three coats of white lead and oil paint should provide this protection for some while.

GESSO. Gesso provides a smooth, firm white surface as a base for bright gilding and polychrome work on a carving. It is especially recommended for carvings made of pine. Errors or small fractures can be modeled up and gesso is good insurance that sap spots will not bleed through the applied finish.

Gesso is a mixture of animal glue, whiting, and water. It can be prepared by heating water in a double boiler, dissolving the glue in the water with occasional stirring, and heating thoroughly. A double boiler must be used, since no glue solution should ever be boiled, overheated, or scorched. Add whiting to the hot glue solution until a thin cream consistency is obtained. I use 3 parts glue to 12 parts water by volume, and 5 parts whiting.

Apply gesso thinly with a brush, in several layers, being careful to use a hot solution. Let each layer dry thoroughly. Enough layers of gesso must be put on the wood so that the final, dried coating can be sandpapered to a smooth finish, free from brushmarks, without the

* Address: Hastings & Co., Inc., 47 West 16th Street, New York 11, N. Y.

sandpaper going through and exposing the wood.   Air bubbles in the first coat should be removed by stroking with your fingertips.   Subsequent coats will conceal any fingermarks.

In this small book on carving I have tried to tell you, in as simple a manner as I could, all the things I have found out about the art in the course of the past years.   I have tried to use words and definitions that make common sense.   I could have used a lot of technical terms that, to the layman at least, would be almost impossible to understand. Knowing that all trades have their own nomenclature, vocabulary and definition, I have tried, by using everyday words, not to confuse the issue.

If I have awakened a desire on your part "to make something," then my efforts have not been in vain. Good Luck!

Glossary

Back Cutting. 1. To carve a detail at an angle from the face—usually done so that the plane of the cut does not show when the carving is viewed vertically. 2. To carve stock away from the back of a carving blank to fit another surface, as in making a stern transom carving.

Band Saw. A power tool that operates an endless steel blade used to cut intricate curves.

Bosting. The first cut made on stock to reduce the piece to a rough approximation of the desired form, thickness, or section.

Brads. Small nails or steel pins.

Burnish. To polish to a high lustre.

Burr. 1. A roughness on a tool handle. 2. A broken edge or end on an edged tool. 3. The wire, i.e., thin portion of steel, that results from sharpening a tool on coarse stone.

Cartouche. An oval, round or other shaped design, usually applied on a surface.

Catheads. Timbers that project beyond the deck and hull of a vessel in the bow for the purpose of lifting the anchor clear of the water.

Chamfer. 1. A sloped or angular surface. 2. A tapered piece. 3. The border of a raised panel.

Checks. In wood, the cracks that occur through improper drying. Usually at the ends of planks or billets.

Chisels. Straight, flat tools with various kinds of cutting edges. Straight: cutting edge is at right angle to long side of tool. Skew: edges are at an angle more than 90° to long side of tool. Usually a chisel has a single heel; a skew, two heels.

Clamps. Any device used to hold stock in place either for glueing or on the bench for working.

Compound Carving. One that is built up of several pieces.

Counterbore. A hole bored into wood with a specially shaped tool bit as described. Its purpose is to locate the head of a wood screw well below the surface of the surrounding material and provide a hole in which a plug can be set.

121

Countersink. A tool made with angular cutting surfaces so that the head of a wood screw can be located slightly below the surface of the surrounding material and the hole filled with plastic wood or the like.

Curl. 1. Swirls or twists in the grain structure of wood. 2. The way a piece of wood will warp.

Detail Carving. The reduction of the bosted, or rough, carving to the desired shape, profile, or detail. The final step in producing the finished carving.

Draw Shave. A steel tool with a long cutting edge and handles set at right angles thereto. Used to reduce edge stock to the desired rough outline or profile.

Driving a Tool. To use a mallet to force the edge of a tool into wood. *Overdrive* means to force the tool into the wood to the point where the cut is too deep and the wood splits or the tool is broken.

Dutchman. A tapered oval piece of wood used as an inlay in repairing a blemish or miscut in the surface of a carving.

Dyes. Colors prepared from chemicals used to dye or change the appearance of stock. (I don't like to use this material, personally.)

Earth Colors. These are finely divided dry colors made from various types of clay or mineral salts or precipitants, usually fired or baked at high heat. These are fast colors, i.e., they never change in color or tone after being exposed to light.

Face Side. That portion of stock that is inside the guide or profile lines and from which the carving is to be made.

Figurehead. A carved design or figure placed on the upper part of a vessel's bow, usually directly below the bowsprit.

Finish. The method and material used to complete the exterior of a carving and to protect it.

Gesso. A mixture of animal glue, water and whiting: about 3 parts glue, 5 parts whiting, 12 parts water, by volume. To make: Heat water in double boiler, melt glue in it, add whiting. Apply with a brush thinly. Used for a base for fine, bright gilding or for polychrome work.

Gilding. The application of gold leaf to a surface. Described at length in Chapter 11.

Gilding Size. *See* Size.

Gilt. A paint. A poor substitute for gold leaf.

Gouges.   The carving tools which, in cross section, are curved to various radii.

Grain.   1. The manner in which the fibres of wood grow.   2. The direction in which the fibres appear to go in a section of wood.

Guide Lines.   Lines drawn on the bosted surface of a carving along which the various tools are to be run for finished carving detail.

Heel.   In woodworking tools, that portion of the tool on its underside at the cutting edge.

Hold-Down.   A piece of plywood screwed to the back of a carving blank; used to hold the blank on the bench top.

Hone.   A fine-grained sharpening stone.   To use a hone: Use water or saliva as a lubricant.   Wipe stone dry when through sharpening tool.

Hot Glue.   Animal glue that must be melted in hot water to use.   Now superseded in most shops by the various synthetic glues that are much faster setting, easier to handle, some being water resisting.   (I do not use instant-setting glue in my work.   I am not in that much of a hurry.)

Index.   1. To indicate the point where adjacent parts of a drawing or carving are to come together and coincide exactly.   2. To mark.

Jack Plane.   A short-bodied hand plane.   *See* Planes.

Jigsaw.   A power tool that is used to cut curves by means of a short blade moving in an up-and-down motion.   Useful for stock up to 1 inch thickness.

Joint.   The art of joining two pieces of wood together.   Edge jointing, face jointing, tenons and dovetails are all methods of joining.

Kiln Dried.   Wood that has been placed in a sealed room and subjected to high, dry heat to remove its moisture.

Lead.   The length of the heel of an edged woodworking tool, i.e., a chisel, gouge, plane iron, and so on.

Lining Out.   Drawing in the guide lines on a carving.

Long Bend, or Bent.   See illustration of the carving tools.   It is easier to see than to describe.   Also short bend, or bent.

Long Lead.   A long tapered edge on woodworking tools.

Mill Planed Stock.   Stock that has been planed at the lumber mill with rotary planers.   These surfaces must always be hand-planed before the stock is either jointed or finished.

Miserere. A bracket under a seat in a church stall on which the clergy can kneel when the seat is turned up.

Mock-up. A temporary form made to represent a finished surface or object as nearly like the original as can be done. Used when the original object cannot be at hand on which to fit a carving.

Motif. The theme. The salient part of a design or work.

Oiling. Application of raw or boiled linseed oil to the finished carving. (I use boiled oil in my work.)

Overcarve, or Overcut. Taking off too much stock in bosting out.

Overlay. Stock that is to be applied to the base to increase its thickness to the desired plane.

Overrun. To carve the finished detail beyond the guide lines, thus carving away stock that should be left for further detail. A good way to spoil a carving.

Panel Raising. That portion of a panel that projects slightly above the chamfered borders; the surface on which a carving is to be made.

Pare. To take light cuts with hand tools. Usually used when speaking of exterior cuts, as when finishing profiles.

Parting Tool. A carving tool with a double-edge shaped in the form of a V, the sides being at several different angles in various numbered tools.

Pierced Carving. A carving that uses holes to emphasize some of the detail. Piercings always go all the way through a carving and are made by boring holes, carving holes, or sawing holes completely through the stock, as laid out in the design.

Pitch Pocket. Sappy inclusion in pine or any resinous wood entirely surrounded by the wood structure.

Planes. 1. The different thicknesses or surfaces of a carving. 2. Hand tools described as follows: Block, 3 to 6 inches long; Fore, 18 inches long; Jack, 14 inches long; Jointer, 21 inches long; Smoother, 9 inches long. The names identify the use. "Fore" is for finishing the face and edge, flat.

Plug Cutter. Specially shaped tool for cutting plugs from wood. Plugs are cut across the grain. Dowels are cut with the grain. This tool will make both.

Polychrome. Many-colored.

Polychroming. The application of paints to a carving.

Profile. 1. The lines scribed or drawn outlining the shape of the carving. 2. The actual outline of a carving after it has been cut from the original stock. Also the outline of another form or object.

Rasp. A coarse-toothed file especially for wood. Very fast cutting. Smaller, specially shaped rasps are called *rifflers*.

Relief. A special form of carving as described in the text.

Relieve. To cut away stock in order to emphasize the detail.

Rifflers. Specially shaped wood rasps for removing stock from difficult places in the carving. Used in place of edged tools at times.

Rope Moulding. A carved section representing the lay of rope. Used mostly for border areas or for contrast with other mouldings.

Rubbed Back. A term applied when the high gloss of varnish finishes is rubbed over with rottenstone (finely divided pumice) and boiled oil to reduce the gloss to a satin-smooth finish.

Run of the Grain. The direction of the grain of the wood.

Sap Streaks. Imperfections found in resinous woods. Streaks of hardened sap or resin most commonly found in white pine; very infrequently found in mahogany.

Scribe. 1. A pencil compass. 2. To mark a line. 3. To indicate a depth for a sinking.

Scrolls. 1. Shaped boards on which running designs are carved. 2. Running designs carved directly on a portion of the carving.

Scroll Saw. A hand tool used to cut intricate curves; sometimes called a *turning saw* or a *coping saw*.

Seal. To fill the wood structure with a foreign material—white lead, lithopone, or the like—to prevent absorption of oils or other vehicles used in finishing processes.

Shakes. Separation of the grain of wood longitudinally, usually the result of high winds twisting trees.

Sinking. Deeply depressed area in a carving.

Size. 1. The application of a specially prepared varnish to the surface of a carving as an adhesive bond for gilding. 2. The slow-set commercial varnish so used.

Skew. 1. At an angle. 2. A specially shaped chisel.

Slips. Specially shaped, small sharpening stones.

Spoke Shave. A steel tool with two handles, about 8 inches long overall, used to make finished cuts on vertical surfaces. It is a tricky tool to use.

Stern Transom. The aftermost portion of a vessel's hull, more or less vertical and slightly rounded, which closes in the hull from one side to the other.

Stone. Usually this term is applied to a fast-cutting emery or Carborundum stone used for sharpening tools.

Stopcuts. Vertical cuts made about the outline of a portion of a carving.

Strop.   A piece of leather loaded with very fine emery powder (#400) used for finish-sharpening edged tools.

Sweeps.   Long, continuous cuts made with a gouge in wood carving.

Tack.   In gilding, the stickiness of the gilding size.

Template.   Usually a thin piece of stock made to fit a surface as exactly as possible from which a duplicate of the original may be made.

Tools.   Generally divided into two categories: hand tools and machine tools. Hand tools are those that are used in the hand of the operator. All carving and most carpenter's tools are in this category. Machine tools are power-driven mechanical aids only and are used primarily to prepare stock for final manipulation with hand tools.

Transfer.   To trace the outline of a drawing on a piece of stock by means of carbon paper placed between the original drawing and the stock, carbon side down preferably.

Transom.   A permanent partition on board ship. *See* Stern Transom.

Vehicle.   The medium or substance in liquid form in which color stock is let down, or mixed. It is usually made of linseed oil, turpentine, varnish, japan, or dryer mixed together in varying proportions.

Vise.   A special device designed to hold work firmly in place between its jaws.

Waste Side.   1. When profiling or cutting out stock for any purpose the waste side is the part of the board or plank *outside* the drawn guide or profile lines. 2. That portion of the stock that is to be cut off or carved off and thrown away.

Web.   That portion of stock left when two or more holes are bored adjacent to but not touching each other, as in making a piercing. *See also* Pierced Carving.

Wind.   A cut made by a carving tool that is being rotated about its longitudinal axis as the tool is "led through" the wood, that is, as the cut is being made.

Ying and Yang.   The Chinese design representing The Life Everlasting.

Index

African mahogany, 8
Alto-relievo, 34, 36, 40, 44, 109
Amazon mahogany, 8
American Eagle, 59, 60
American vermilion, 113, 114
American walnut, 5, 7
Aronson, Joseph, vi
Axis, 64

Back-cut, 4, 58, 73, 80, 89, 92, 94, 95, 104
Back saw, 22, 76, 102
Back up, 55
Band saw, 22, 47, 48
Banners, 89, 91
Base block, 59
Bas relief, 36, 44, 82, 91, 106, 108
Baxter State Park, 61
Beak, 38
Bellamy, John, v
Bench carving, 29
Bit brace, 21, 70
Blank, 58
Block, 89–96
Board, 117
Body pad, 44
Bookcase, 109
Bost, 50, 55–58, 62, 65, 72, 73, 75, 91, 92, 106, 107
Bottoming, 5, 6, 91
Bottom rest, 38
Bremen Eagle, 44
British Admiralty, v
Broad gouge, 64, 65
Brush (camel's hair, red badger, squirrel), 117
Burnt Sienna, 113
Burnt Umber, 113
Burr, 16

Cameo, 36
Carbon paper, 45

Carpenter's compass, **22**
Carpenter's scribe, 22
Carving block, 9, 40, 45, 46
Cartouche, 2
Casemaker's square, 22
Catheads, 2
Centerline, 38, 40
Cere, 38
Chamfer, 58
Chase, Charles G., 84, 85
Checks, 12
Chest, 19, 32
Chisel, 13, 14, 17, 56
Chord, 93, 94
Christensen, Erwin O., v
Clamp, 50, 52, 53, 55, 62, 98
Claw hammer, 21
Clip, 9
Clipped ends, 53
Cobb, Gerald, v
Color stock, 113
Commercial stains, 114
Compound carvings, 34, 44, 46, 59, 71
Corner cupboard, 108
Counterbore, 21, 29, 50, 59, 95, 98
Countersink, 21, 50
Crest, 38
Cross-cut saw, 22
Cross section, 40, 102

Damariscotta, Maine, 62
Damon, Harry F., 42
Day, Maurice ("Jake"), 60–62
Design, 36, 44, 49, 57
Detail, 36, 40, 56, 73
Dolan, Patrick, facing Page 1
Dolphin, 73, 91, 94
Drafting, 33
Draw shave, 66, 92, 93
Drawing, 36, 38, 40, 44–46, 76, 95
Drawing board, 33, 38

127

Drawing paper, 36, 92, 93
Drawing table, 33
Drill, 21, 50, 59
Drill press, 23
Drive, 64
Dry color (earthen), 113
Dryer (Japan), 113
Duco cement, 99
Dutchman, 7

Eagle, 38, 59–62, 64, 70, 73, 78
Earthen colors, 113
Edge, 64
Encyclopaedia Britannica, v
"Encyclopedia of Furniture," v
End grain, 83
Everdure, 98
Exterior cuts, 48
Eye, 38

Face of tool, 107
Feather, feathers, feathering, 38, 73, 75, 76, 84
Feet, 38
Ferrule, 64
Figureheads, American, and their Carvers, v
Figure heads, American, and their Carvers, v
Figureheads, 2
Files (see Rasps and rifflers)
Finish, 112
Finish carve, 92
Finishing cuts, 83, 104
Finishing tools, 73
Fire frame, 111
Firmer chisel, 103, 104
Fluter, 109
Freeman, Mrs. E. R., 69
Frye, Mrs. Carl R., 46

Gesso, 7, 118
Gibbons, Grinling, v
Gild, 117
Gilder's size, 116
Gilder's tip, 117
Gilding, 112, 116–118
Gilt paint, 112
Gold leaf, 116
Gouges, 13, 14, 19, 56, 76
Grain, 44
Graves, Mortimer, 67

Guide lines, 44, 73, 78, 104
Gulf of Mexico, 61

Hand drill, 21
Hand, George, 60–62
Hand plane, 52
Handle, 64
Hastings & Co., 116
Head, 38, 44
Heel, 17
Hemlock, 29
Henning, Dr. R. B., 81
High detail, 56
Hold-down, 55, 57, 64, 70, 72
Holidays, 116
Honduras mahogany, 9
Hone, 18

Index, 38, 50, 101, 104
Indian red, 113
Intaglio, 36, 109
Interior cuts, 48

Jack knife, 1, 20
Jack plane, 20
Japan, 113, 116
Jig saw, 48
Joining, 44
Joint, 49, 51, 92, 94, 96
Jointed, 59
Jointer, 22, 52
Jointing, 52
Jointing plane, 20

Katahdin, 61
Kiln (dry), 9, 12
Knots, 102
Kokua (ketch), 97

Lapping compound, 18
Layout, 36
Layout drawing, 36
Layout lines, 102
Layout sketch, 36
Lead, 7
Life magazine, 2
Lignum vitae, 16
Lining out, 73
Linseed oil, 113, 116
Livingston, Stanley, Jr., 97
Long bend (or bent), 13, 104
Lotus flower, 109

Lynch, Rev. G. Ernest, 45
Lynn Historical Society, 79

McIntire, Samuel, v, 79
Mahogany, 4, 5, 8, 9, 82
Maine Coast Fisherman, 8, 15, 57
Malden National Bank, 42
Mallet, 16
Mantel shelf, 111
Man-trap, 48
Masking tape, 93
Merrill, Richard, 79
Mezzo-relievo, 36, 91, 94, 109
Mill planed, 51
Miserere, 2
Mock-up, 92, 93, 95
Model, 56, 106, 107
Mounted leaf, 117

Nail set, 21
"National Geographic Magazine," vi
Nostril, 38

Oil, linseed, 113
"Old Churches of London," v
Outline, 38, 82, 93, 95, 101, 107
Outline cuts, 78, 107
Overcarve, 59
Overcut, 56
Overlap, 93, 107
Overlay, 50
Overrun, 75

Paint, 112, 115
Panel, 73, 101, 102, 104
Panel saw, 102
Parting tool, 12, 13, 15, 73, 76, 78
Patina, 112
Payne, U. S. Senator Frederick G., 78
Pencil, 33
Pierce, 48, 67, 68, 70, 71
Pigment, 114
Pineapple, 101, 102, 104, 106, 108, 109
Pinckney, Pauline A., v
Pitch pocket, 7
Plane (face or surface), 40, 56, 59, 73, 76, 94, 102
Plane (tool), 20
Plastic seal, 98
Plug, 21, 29, 44, 50, 51, 96, 99
Plug cutters, 21
Plywood, 33, 93
Polychrome, 112, 114

Portland Press-Herald, 60
Power arm, 65
Price, Drs. Roland and Mary, 46
Prime coating, 114
Profile, 47–49, 55, 58, 70, 72, 92, 93, 95
Profile cuts, 80

Radius, 92
Raising, 102–104
Rasp, 28, 71, 90
Raw Sienna, 113
Raw Umber, 113, 114
Relief carving (forms of), 36, 76, 109
Riffled, 9
Rifflers, 22, 28, 71, 90, 96
Rolling Stone IV, 3
Rope molding, 76, 108
Run of the grain, 75
Running out, 80, 83

Salem Eagle, 70
Sandpaper, 83, 108
Sap streaks, 102
Scallop shell, 110
Screw, 59, 92, 95, 96
Screw driver, 21
Scribe (tool), 56, 89, 91–93, 95
Scroll saw, 21, 47, 49
Sculpture Associates, 25–27, 65
Seal, 114
Section lines, 101
Shakes, 12, 102
Sharpening, 17
Shellac, 93
Short bend (bent), 13
Short set, 113
Sinkings, 70
Size, 116, 117
Sketch, 62
Skew chisel, 5, 13, 14, 15, 17, 76, 77, 78, 104-106
Skillin, Simeon, v
Skips, 118
Slips, 17
Slow set, 116
South Bristol, Maine, 109
Southworth, William, v
Spokeshave, 22, 66, 92, 93
Sponge rubber, 96
Squier, Joel, H., 74, 98
Stain, 112–114
State Seals, 112
Stern transom, 87–98

Stewart, Glenn, 37, 39, 111
Stone, 16, 17
Stone, Donald, 3
Stopcuts, 6, 56, 57, 70, 91, 104, 105
Straight, 13
Straight edge, 22, 57
Strop, 16, 17
Sweep, 7, 84
Synthetic materials, 115

Table saw, 22
Tack, 116
Tang, 18, 64
Template, 92, 93
Tenoning saw, 22, 102
Terminal leaves, 104
Thompson, W. D., Jr., 45
Tools,
    carpenter's, 20
    hand, 20
    machine, 22, 23
Tool rack, 32
Tool tray, 20
Tracing paper, 38
Transfer, 47, 93
Transom (*see* Stern transom)
Tube color, 113

Turning saw, 20
Turpentine, 113, 116

Valance boards, 110
Van Dyke brown, 113, 114
Vehicle, 113, 115
Viking, v
Vise, 30, 31
Vise jig, 63, 64

Waldoboro, Maine, 60
Walnut, 7
Waste stock, 22, 47, 56, 75
Watertight joint, 98
Web, 70
Weldwood glue, 54
White lead, 115, 116
White oak, 5
White pine, 7, 102
Wings, 38, 59, 84
Wood joiner, 92
Wood rasp, 22
Wood screws, 44, 92
Working drawing, 40, 45, 73, 75

Yacht, 2, 87, 93, 94
Yachting Magazine, 96, 97
Ying and Yang, 108